Essays in Criticism
and
Literary Theory

Crofts Classics

JOSEPH ADDISON

Essays in Criticism and Literary Theory

edited by
John Loftis
Stanford University

AHM Publishing Corporation
Northbrook, Illinois 60062

ISBN: 0-88295-106-8

Library of Congress Card Number: 74-76968

PRINTED IN THE UNITED STATES OF AMERICA
715

Contents

Introduction   1

Principal Dates in the Life of Joseph Addison .. 16

HUMOR

    Spectator, No. 35.   False humor and true
                            humor 18
    Spectator, No. 47.   The psychology of humor   22
    Spectator, No. 249. Uses and abuses of
                            ridicule 26

TRAGEDY

    Spectator, No. 39.   The language of tragedy   30
    Spectator, No. 40.   Objections to "poetical
                            justice" in tragedy 34
    Spectator, No. 42.   The staging of tragedy ... 39
    Spectator, No. 44.   The depiction of violence
                            in tragedy 42
    Spectator, No. 548. Objections to "poetical
                            justice" clarified 48

TRUE AND FALSE WIT

    Spectator, No. 58.   Varieties of false wit 53
    Spectator, No. 59.   Varieties of false wit 57
    Spectator, No. 60.   Varieties of false wit 62
    Spectator, No. 61.   False wit: punning 67
    Spectator, No. 62.   True wit, mixed wit,
                            and false wit 71
    Spectator, No. 63.   The forms of wit: an
                            allegorical analysis....... 77

BALLADS

Spectator, No. 70.   *Chevy Chase* and
                       epic tradition 83
Spectator, No. 74.   *Chevy Chase* and
                       the *Aeneid* 90
Spectator, No. 85.   *Two Children in the
                       Wood* 96

GENIUS

Spectator, No. 160. The nature of genius ... 100

MILTON

Spectator, No. 267. The "fable" of *Paradise
                       Lost* 104
Spectator, No. 273. The characters of
                       Paradise Lost 108
Spectator, No. 279. The "sentiments" of
                       Paradise Lost 113
Spectator, No. 285. The language of
                       Paradise Lost 118
Spectator, No. 291. *Paradise Lost* and the
                       art of criticism 124
Spectator, No. 297. The faults of *Paradise
                       Lost* 128

TASTE

Spectator, No. 409. The nature of taste in
                       literary criticism 134

THE PLEASURES OF THE IMAGINATION

Spectator, No. 411. Introductory 138

Spectator, No. 412. Pleasures of the imagination derived from the great, the uncommon, and the beautiful 141

Spectator, No. 413. Divine purpose responsible for the pleasures of the imagination 146

Spectator, No. 414. Nature and art as sources of the pleasures of the imagination 149

Spectator, No. 415. Architecture as a source of the pleasures of the imagination 152

Spectator, No. 416. The secondary pleasures of the imagination 158

Spectator, No. 417. Pleasures of the imagination arising from the association of ideas . 162

Spectator, No. 418. Pleasures of the imagination arising from the literary experience of terror and pity 166

Spectator, No. 419. Pleasures of the imagination arising from "the fairy way of writing" 170

Spectator, No. 420. Pleasures of the imagination arising from scientific observation ... 173

Spectator, No. 421. Pleasures of the imagination arising from rhetorical artifice 176

DRAMATIC REFORM

Spectator, No. 446. Licentiousness in the
                           drama and the need
                           for supervision of the
                           theaters 183

Bibliography 187

Introduction

Virginia Woolf, who has some claim to be considered the best essayist of the twentieth century, was temperate in her praise of Addison, who may more confidently be judged the best essayist of the eighteenth century. "Neither lusty nor lively," she wrote in 1919, "is the adjective we should apply to the present condition of the *Tatler* and the *Spectator*." Yet if his best work, a series of essays contributed to *The Spectator*, has lost some of its former popularity, good reasons remain, now as at any other time, for reading it. The journal is above all famous for the completeness with which it records the life of Queen Anne's England: what men talked about and thought on many subjects, including literature and literary criticism. In it Addison provided a systematic exposition of critical assumptions that shaped eighteenth-century literature, as well as numerous anticipations of those that influenced the literature of a later time.

He wrote essays on *Paradise Lost*, a poem resembling classical models; and he wrote essays on "the pleasures of the imagination," trying to assimilate the empirical and conceptual discoveries of near-contemporary philosophers and show their relevance to aesthetics. The latter essays, summarizing theories that anticipate romanticism, are as psychological in their concern with the experience of art as the essays on *Paradise Lost* are formalistic, preoccupied with the structure of the poem and its resemblance to other epics. Addison was eclectic in his approach to literary problems. He was sensitive to Hobbes's and Locke's investigations in philosophy and psychology, and in following them he expressed attitudes that found fulfillment in romantic critical theory. Yet he remained a neoclassicist. Repeatedly he invoked the principle of uniformity: the assumption, fundamental to neoclassical theory, that men are everywhere alike

1

and hence that literature everywhere has common subjects and common strategies. He could compare the ballad of *Chevy Chase* to the *Aeneid* without assuming that the anonymous poet had any knowledge of Vergil. Repeatedly he cited the literature of classical antiquity as a measure of excellence. And repeatedly he stressed the didactic in neo-classical theory—understandably in his discussion of the need for dramatic reform (no. 446) and even in his essays on the meanings of critical terms such as *humor* and *wit*.

The usefulness of the essays is enhanced for us by the fact that they are concerned with principles applicable to many works rather than with the detailed analysis of a few single works. Searching for permanent truths about literature, Addison proceeded on a level of generalization. Even the essays on individual poems, on *Paradise Lost*, for example, or on the ballad of *Chevy Chase*, depart from the specific, so pronounced is the generalizing habit of mind. The first of the essays on *Chevy Chase* (no. 70) begins with a succinct statement of the principle of uniformity in aesthetics and then moves on to illustrate that principle in the folk ballad. This method of organization is typical of the essays: the careful enunciation of a principle—whether about uniformity of taste, as here, or about poetic justice or wit or humor—followed by its elucidation in examples. He was as much concerned with universals as was, in his separate way and later generation, Samuel Johnson.

In his essay on taste (no. 409) Addison describes the pattern he envisions as linking the critical essays. He has already endeavored, he writes, to detect "several of those false kinds [of wit] which have been admired in the different ages of the world and at the same time to show wherein the nature of true wit consists." He has pointed out (in his essays on *Chevy Chase*) "the great force which lies in a natural simplicity of thought." And he has given attention as well to Milton, "the greatest poet which our nation or perhaps any other has produced." In the series of essays on *Paradise Lost*, he has "particularized most of those rational and manly beauties which give a value to that divine work." He now proposes to consider at large "the pleasures of the imagination" and to suggest "what it is that gives a beauty to many passages of the finest writers both in prose and verse." He omits reference to the essays on tragedy, and he may imply a greater orderliness of design among the groups of essays than exists. His statement provides, however, his own warrant for our regarding the body of criticism as a coherent whole, and it conveys his sense of the corrective purpose of the essays. Like *The Tatler* before it, *The Spectator* was a contribution to the reform movement of early eighteenth-century England; and the essays from *The Spectator* collected here represent an extension of the movement into aesthetics. They were instructional in intent, an effort to enlarge the subjects of literary appreciation, to provide critical terminology for the discussion of literature, and to clarify the criteria by which it was to be judged.

Addison's theatrical criticism reveals his philosophical turn of mind, his preference for general principles over detailed analysis. His preoccupation with first principles is the more notable in this instance because it stands in contrast with the practice of Steele, who customarily wrote about plays that had recently been or were about to be performed. Steele was a journalistic critic of the theater, the first important one in England; Addison, on the other hand, was a dramatic theorist. At the time of *The Spectator*, Steele had written three plays, and he was long and well acquainted with the leading actors, whose performances provided the subjects of some of his essays. Addison had not yet completed his first play, and he did not habitually go to the theater. When he writes about a current theatrical issue—in the essay on the dramatic reform movement (no. 446), for example—he promptly introduces comparisons with the drama of antiquity and relates current practice to neoclassical theory: in this instance, to the obligation of the dramatist to instruct as well as entertain his audience. His remarks on English dramatists and their plays, though well informed and illuminating, are typically brief *obiter dicta*, such as the comments on Nathaniel Lee and Thomas Otway in no. 39.

Addison's four essays on tragedy (nos. 39, 40, 42, and 44) appeared in April 1711, just two years before the first performance of his own tragedy, *Cato*, in April 1713. At the time he wrote the essays he had already written most of the tragedy. We are thus justified in scrutinizing them for in-

sight into the principles that shaped the play. *Cato* proved to
be, in the restricted sense of its fortune on the stage, a
preeminently successful adaptation of French conceptions
of dramatic form. Addison's recommendation (in no. 39) of
"a noble sentiment," together with his criticism of English
dramatists for indulgence in the "very trifling or very common," indicates the frame of mind that led to the preter-
natural earnestness of the play: its sentiments are so noble
that the characters who express them lose psychological
plausibility. And his further recommendation (in no. 44),
that displays of violent action before an audience be sharply
reduced or eliminated, is an expression of the theory that
generated long passages of expository narration in *Cato*.
Addison presumably thought that he was providing the
kind of neoclassical tragedy of strong good sense, undam-
aged by melodramatic spectacle, that he had recommended
in his essays.

His discussion of "poetical justice" (in no. 40) also seems
relevant to *Cato*. The title character of the play, though a
figure of legendary nobility and virtue, meets his death by
suicide, as the army of the victorious Caesar approaches. It
would appear that Addison, not convinced by current arguments in support of poetic justice, undertook in *The
Spectator* to justify the catastrophe he planned for his still
unfinished tragedy. In any event, both the essay on poetic
justice and the exemplification of it in the tragedy two years
later brought him under severe and telling attack from the
most acute and systematic of his contemporary critics, John
Dennis. Addison's remarks on poetic justice show an unre-
solved tension between empirically observed life, on the
one hand, and, on the other, the orderly and just nature
which, according to many theorists, the poet should imitate.

John Dennis was prompt to remind Addison of his incon-
sistencies. In a letter *To the Spectator, Upon His Paper on the
16th of April*, Dennis used in rebuttal both authority (most
notably, Aristotle) and systematic argument. "For what
tragedy can there be without a fable," Dennis asks rhetori-
cally, "or what fable without a moral, or what moral without
poetical justice; what moral, where the good and the bad are
confounded by destiny, and perish alike promiscuously?"
In *The Spectator* no. 548, Addison attempts to vindicate his

original position by redefining it. Dennis, citing Aristotle, had insisted that only an imperfect man was a fit protagonist for tragedy, since only such a man could be subjected to catastrophe without damage to the didactic effectiveness of the play. Now Addison (or some unidentified collaborator) argued that any man—an exceptionally good as well as an imperfect man—has enough of evil about him to qualify for the role of tragic hero: "our goodness being of a comparative and not an absolute nature." Perhaps a certain amount of sophistry appears in this later essay; at any rate, it reveals clearly enough that Dennis had scored and that Addison or his defender was attempting to reinterpret his position in a manner approximating the position held by Dennis.

Among the most influential of the essays—and the most productive of literary results—is the series on ballads (nos. 70, 74, and 85). These essays provide a rationale for, and to a limited extent are a cause of, the antiquarian movement that found expression later in the century in collections of folk ballads such as those of Allan Ramsay, Bishop Percy, and Joseph Ritson and in imitations of primitive poetry such as those of Thomas Gray, Thomas Chatterton, and William Wordsworth. Although others before Addison had admired and praised ballads (he names Sidney, Jonson, Dryden, and the Earl of Dorset), he was the first to provide a systematic defense of them and to make an interest in them fashionable. Conservative and at the same time innovative in their implications, these essays show Addison's characteristic use of classical literature as a measure of greatness even as they show him searching for excellence in literature isolated from classical tradition. The rationalistic basis of his neoclassicism is nowhere more evident than here in his appeal to the literary experience of all men in all places and times: in his assumption that, insofar as men think justly about literature, they think alike. There is a bold democracy of aesthetic theory in these essays, bolder in fact than some of Addison's distinguished contemporaries were willing to accept.

Later in the century, Samuel Johnson, along with many others, dissented; in Addison's time John Dennis did so, writing a rebuttal in the form of an epistle: *To H — C — Esq; Of Simplicity in Poetical Compositions, in Remarks on the 70th*

Spectator. Dennis's essay focuses on Addison's theoretical groundwork. Addison had praised the simple and un-adorned style of the ballads and had assumed that the un-learned taste of common folk could be just. Dennis invokes the doctrine of original sin. Before the Fall the untutored human mind might have been a reliable guide, but not now in its actual state of degeneracy. He describes tellingly the vulgarity of entertainments enjoyed by uneducated people. And he finds Addison's praise of the simple ballad style unacceptable, objecting—most of us would say under-standably—to the comparison of *Chevy Chase* to the *Aeneid*. To Addison's stylistic analysis of *Chevy Chase* (no. 74), which was intended to support his claim that "there are several parts in it where not only the thought but the lan-guage is majestic and the numbers sonorous," Dennis re-plies with incredulity and with a reconsideration of the components of poetic style. Dennis could no more consider primitive poetry comparable to the best poetry of sophisti-cated civilization than could Samuel Johnson.

We are not free from the prejudices of our own time, but we have the perspective of distance, and on this issue we think that we can see more clearly than the critics of the eighteenth century. Addison was right, of course, that bal-lads merited collection and study, and we may be grateful for the stimulus he provided to the antiquarian movement that led to their preservation, even while we read the cau-tions and dissents of Dennis and Johnson with amused half-belief.

The essays on the pleasures of the imagination were probably written as a single unit and certainly should be studied as such. They reveal, like many of the essays, tradi-tional ideas brought into conjunction with ideas derived from Addison's innovative speculations and from his read-ing in the works of near-contemporary theorists: in this instance, notably of John Locke. Addison includes theologi-cal arguments that can be traced to the middle ages or even to antiquity. In no. 413 he comments: "The Supreme Author of our being has so formed the soul of man that nothing but himself can be its last, adequate, and proper happiness," a statement that in its appeal to a final cause or purpose amidst an analytical discussion of aesthetics is scarcely compatible with the mode of investigation the Royal Society had advocated since the Restoration. Yet Addison makes use of Newton's optical theory and Locke's related distinction between primary and secondary qualities. "I have here supposed," he writes in no. 413, referring to the second book of Locke's *Essay Concerning Human Understanding*, "that my reader is acquainted with that great modern discovery, which is at present universally acknowledged by all the enquirers into natural philosophy; namely, that light and colors, as apprehended by the imagination, are only ideas in the mind and not qualities that have any existence in matter." Throughout the series he focuses attention on the interaction between the external world and what passes within the mind, using Lockeian terminology and discriminations in support of his assertion of the divine purpose responsible for man's aesthetic responses. Like many of his contemporaries, he subordinated philosophical speculation to Christianity.

However striking are the anticipations, in the essays on the imagination, of the themes of later eighteenth-century romanticism, Addison is thoroughly of his time in a fundamental aspect of his investigation: attention to the psychology of aesthetic response rather than to that of artistic creation. Addison is preoccupied with the *pleasures* of the imagination; not, as was Coleridge a century later, with the shaping and creative force of the imagination. He writes as a connoisseur of sensory impressions, above all visual impressions, rather than as an investigator of the creative process. He thinks of a cultivated imagination as a gentlemanly accomplishment productive of pleasure to its possessor; not as a force that can yield new insight into truth. Insofar as he alludes to the process of artistic creation in the essays, his conception of it is (to use the metaphors described by Professor M. H. Abrams) that of the mirror rather than of the lamp, the conception implied in Pope's definition of wit in his *Essay on Criticism*, published just the year before the essays on the imagination.

The series on the imagination reads like a handbook for the themes and literary strategies of eighteenth-century romanticism: for the poems of Mark Akenside, Joseph Warton, Thomas Warton the Younger, William Collins, and Thomas Gray, among others. Akenside acknowledges his literary debt in the title of his poem, *The Pleasures of Imagination* (1744), a versified extension of Addison's praise of the "high capacious powers" which are "folded up in man." Joseph Warton's debt to Addison in *The Enthusiast: Or, The Lover of Nature* (1744) is perhaps even more comprehensive than Akenside's. The theme of Warton's poem can be summarized in a sentence from *The Spectator*, no. 414: "There is something more bold and masterly in the rough careless strokes of nature than in the nice touches and embellishments of art." And in his illustration of the theme, Warton, like Addison before him, took an image from contrasting landscapes, preferring "some pine-topped precipice / Abrupt and shaggy" to the formal gardens of Versailles. In no. 414 Addison had written that he "would rather look upon a tree in all its luxuriancy and diffusion of boughs and branches than when it is . . . cut and trimmed into a mathematical figure." Warton's pejorative reference to "the lays of artful Addison / Coldly correct" has a note of ironic incongruity about it, so thoroughly had Addison himself anticipated the critical stance implied in Warton's comparison of *Cato* and Shakespeare's plays.

The essays on the imagination provide a rationale for the romantic poems of the mid-century: for their organization not as logically structured statements but as evocations, by way of striking sensory images, of a succession of moods. Like the essays, the poems have a strain of hedonism, a strain of self-indulgent connoisseurship of sensations, including sensations that in the eighteenth century were associated with the "sublime": that is, with an elevation—or ecstasy—of spirit evoked by passionate and awe-inspiring experience, such as can result from the sight of "some pine-topped precipice / Abrupt and shaggy." Nos. 412 and 418 anticipate important conceptions in Burke's *Philosophical Inquiry into the Sublime and Beautiful* (1756). Addison resembles the mid-century poets (as well as much older theorists) in his emphasis on the visual. "Our sight is the most perfect of all our senses," he asserts at the beginning of the first essay in the series: "It fills the mind with the largest variety of ideas, converses with its objects at the greatest distance, and continues the longest in action without being tired or satiated with its proper enjoyments," a statement which may be read as an epigraph for a body of poetry with so prominent a component of visual imagery as that of the eighteenth-century romantics. By way of "similitudes, metaphors, and allegories" in poetry, as Addison explains in no. 421, "a truth in the understanding is as it were reflected by the imagination; we are able to see something like color and shape in a notion and to discover a scheme of thoughts traced out upon matter." The personified abstractions of eighteenth-century poetry (to which Wordsworth was to take exception much later) could be justified—in critical theory at any rate—as a means of rendering the abstract perceptible to the senses.

Addison recognized inadequacies in the eighteenth-century critical vocabulary at about the same time as Pope did in *An Essay on Criticism*. Several of the essays were devoted to an effort to give such terms as *wit*, *humor*, *taste*, and *genius* a more precise meaning. But he was more confident than we are that abstract terms referring to the faculties (as in his playful genealogy of *humor* in no. 35) are meaningful. What he calls (in no. 47) a "more philosophical language" than common speech consists essentially of generalized terms about human emotions and faculties. Yet if we read him with an awareness of change in critical terminology, we can find in the essays a neatly articulated expression of several Augustan attitudes.

One of the most illustrious of the Queen Anne wits, writing two generations after Hobbes's analysis of wit and the Restoration comedy of wit, Addison provides a survey of definitions of that elusive and ambiguous term, which was used by the Augustans in a spectrum of meanings. He does not have a semanticist's or even a lexicographer's sense of discriminations, but he makes some useful distinctions nevertheless: the distinction in no. 62, for example, between true and false wit. In his extended discussion of the abuses of wit (in punning, for example), we find a preliminary statement of much that is distinctive in Samuel Johnson's criticism. The essays on wit—however casual, conversational, metaphorical, and even allegorical —articulate major themes of eighteenth-century criticism. We might indeed have a higher regard for the essays had not later critics, above all Johnson, elaborated the themes with more precision and authority.

The essay on taste (no. 409) reveals him preoccupied, as in the series on the imagination, with the psychology of the perception of literature: this time with the task, so difficult in neoclassical theory, of establishing a viable criterion by which literature can be evaluated. The "mechanical rules," as Addison and every other good neoclassical critic realized, were not enough. The observation of them might be a pre-condition of success, but could not ensure success. Pope had said as much the year before in *An Essay on Criticism*—a poem that, like Addison's essay, describes the skills and the qualities of mind requisite to the art of criticizing literature justly. In both works, the remarks tangential to the subject are better than the frontal assaults on it. When Addison attempts a definition of taste, he is at his overconfident worst. He begs the question by restating its terms: "I think I may define it to be that faculty of the soul which discerns the beauties of an author with pleasure and the imperfections with dislike." But if he could not provide a satisfactory definition, neither did anyone else, and in fact the effort to do so rested on the dubious assumption that there was a single "faculty of the soul" to be defined. Still, Addison isolates a methodological problem of criticism, he makes practical suggestions for solving it, and he calls a roll of critics, notably French seventeenth-century critics, who are important to those who would understand the antecedents of English neoclassicism. Even as he names the major French formalist critics, he pays his reverence to Longinus, the presumed author of *On the Sublime*, in whose theories the emphasis on emotional impact over rules is difficult to reconcile with French neoclassicism. Addison thus reminds us that English criticism had two different, and not al-together compatible, strains.

His essay on genius (no. 160) complements the essay on taste and the series on the imagination. Typically, he de-votes twelve essays to the psychology of aesthetic percep-tion and only one to the psychology of artistic creation. On the subject of genius he is brief and less explicit than we could wish. Indeed, our special interest in the essay is partly fortuitous, for we read it not so much for the illumination he provides on the nature of genius as for the importance the subject assumes in the writings of later theorists. Here in *The Spectator* is an early formulation of what was to be one of the major preoccupations of eighteenth- and early nineteenth-century aesthetics, which found its final statement in Coleridge's *Biographia Literaria*. Long before Edward Young's *Conjectures on Original Composition* (1759) and William Duff's *Essay on Original Genius* (1767), Addison expresses the notion that genius possesses a spontaneous creative force, intuitive in its nature and not dependent on training for its achievement. A similar reverence for the power of genius is latent in seventeenth-century discussions of Shakespeare—Dryden's, for example, in *Of Dramatic Poesy*. Dryden had referred to Shakespeare as "the man who of all modern, and perhaps ancient, poets had the largest and most comprehensive soul," and it would appear from the context of the metaphorical word "soul" that Dryden understood by it something not unlike Addison's conception of a genius of the first class (no. 160):

> Among great geniuses those few draw the admiration
> of all the world upon them and stand up as the prod-
> igies of mankind who by the mere strength of natural
> parts and without any assistance of art or learning
> have produced works that were the delight of their
> own times and the wonder of posterity.

This statement is less metaphorical and more analytical than Dryden's—or than those of other seventeenth-century critics—and it advanced understanding of the conception. Addison's illustrations of genius—Homer, poets of the Old Testament, Shakespeare—became conventional later in the eighteenth century, to such an extent that if we come to his essay after extensive reading in later eighteenth-century literature, we may credit him with less originality than he deserves.

The mid-century poets presumably read Addison's essays on Milton as attentively as they read those on the pleasures of the imagination. In any event, Addison was a major popularizer of Milton; and poets who wrote in blank verse from James Thomson onward used Miltonic diction and, to a lesser extent, themes. The grandeur of description in *Paradise Lost* is formative in *The Seasons*, and the cultivated melancholy of *Il Penseroso* is widely echoed, with amplification, in poems of the 1740s and 1750s.

Addison shares prominence with Dennis in early Milton criticism. Although Addison was more widely read and more influential in gaining for *Paradise Lost* the audience it deserved, Dennis's work preceded that of Addison by some two decades. Indeed, Dennis's admiration for Milton, if not his detailed analysis, had been anticipated in the Restoration. In a published letter, dated December 9, 1721, Dennis expresses pique that "some persons" (meaning Addison) borrowed without acknowledgment from his treatises on *Paradise Lost*; and he looks back over his long preoccupation with the poem:

> I believe . . . that I, who have all my lifetime had the highest esteem for the great geniuses of the ancients, and especially for Homer and Vergil, and who admire them now more than ever, have yet for these last thirty years admired Milton above them all for one thing, and this is for having carried away the prize of sublimity from both ancients and moderns; and in most of the treatises which I have published for thirty years . . . I have not been able to forbear pointing at several of the matchless beauties of Milton.

A justifiable boast—and a justifiable reprimand, by indirection, to Addison, whose criticism of Milton is indeed indebted to Dennis. Although Addison is less insistent than Dennis on the sublimity of Milton, he does praise *Paradise Lost* for that quality, and he, too, audaciously prefers Milton to Homer and Vergil.

The essays on *Paradise Lost* provide an extended example of neoclassical critical method: the application of a systematic mode of procedure derived from ancient criticism, as well as the use of ancient literature as a criterion of excellence. Addison alludes to modern critics—to Boileau, Le Bossu, Perrault, and Dryden, among others—as well as borrowing from Dennis. Yet he is most respectful to the critics of antiquity, to Horace and Longinus as well as to Aristotle. He consciously follows the example of Aristotle: "We have already taken a general survey of the fable and characters in Milton's *Paradise Lost*," he writes at the beginning of the third essay (no. 279) in the series; "the parts which remain to be considered, according to Aristotle's method, are the sentiments and the language." He proceeds systematically, perhaps even pedantically, through these aspects of *Paradise Lost*, at every step using comparisons with Homer and Vergil to illuminate his argument. His special tribute to the poem is that he, like Dennis before him, believes *Paradise Lost* can support detailed comparison with the *Iliad* and the *Aeneid*—the English poem in some qualities surpassing, in others falling below, the classical poems. The completeness of Milton's own classicism contributed to the fervor of Addison's admiration for him; significantly, Addison alludes to Shakespeare in this series only tangentially, and links him with Nathaniel Lee as an author in whom "the affectation of greatness often hurts the perspicuity of the style" (no. 285). Shakespeare idolatry was a generation in the future; at the moment, in the stricter classical temper of Queen Anne's England, Milton was supreme.

Distant enough from Milton to be free of political animosities, Addison was yet close enough to him, to his literary culture and his patterns of theological thought, to appreciate his achievement fully. He has little to say about Milton's theology; he acknowledges (no. 267) the incongruity of the adjective *heroic* with Milton's subject but declines to explore the significance of Milton's transvaluation of epic conventions. Unlike Johnson later in the century, he has no misgivings about the propriety of the use of the Christian subject. Rather, he regards Milton's subject as superior to those of the *Iliad* and the *Aeneid* (no. 267): " . . . I think we may say without derogating from those wonderful performances that there is an unquestionable magnificence in every part of *Paradise Lost* and indeed a much greater than could have been formed upon any pagan system." Perhaps Addison had an advantage over Johnson as a critic of Milton: he was a Whig and his religion was more rational, less emotional, than Johnson's. In any event, he provided in these essays a firm base for the national self-congratulation on having produced an epic rivaling those of antiquity.

Several times I have referred to the opposition between Addison and Dennis: to Dennis's anticipation of Addison's admiring criticism of *Paradise Lost*, to Dennis's attacks on Addison's theories about the ballad and poetic justice, to Dennis's censorious review of *Cato*. It is curious that the two men, who in retrospect seem the most considerable critics of

Queen Anne's England, should so often have been an-
tagonists.

The explanation for their disagreements lies perhaps in
their personalities and social positions rather than in their
ideas. In 1711 and 1712 the contrast between them, their
manners of life and their personal appearances, must have
been striking: Addison, a handsome man just forty years
old, socially and politically prominent, already famous;
Dennis, fifty-five and not handsome, poor, and, as a conventional representative of the critic, becoming a favorite
target of abuse. Small wonder that he was irascible and
resentful, and that he was quick to strike when Addison
turned a vulnerable side to him. Addison was vulnerable in
Cato, just as he was ungenerous in failing to acknowledge
Dennis's priority in Milton criticism. In all this we can catch
a glimpse of the qualities that evoked Pope's famous and
devastating portrait of Addison as Atticus in his *Epistle to
Dr. Arbuthnot*.

Addison and Dennis, in their critical positions, were both
liberal neoclassicists. Each in his own way attempted to
reconcile a critical doctrine grounded in ancient theory, and
reinforced by Italian and French interpreters of classical
literature, with strongly held personal tastes in literature.
We note differences in emphasis in their critical
works—Dennis's deeper commitment to the Longinian
conception of the sublime, for example; and we note more
emphatic differences in their critical styles: Dennis's the
more tightly argued and systematic, Addison's the more
discursive, graceful, and ingratiating. Dennis was perhaps
the more original and audacious; Addison was certainly the
more widely read and influential.

This edition follows, as copy text, a set of the original folio
half sheets now in the Henry E. Huntington Library. The
text has been corrected in accordance with the lists of errata
included by the original printers. Spelling and punctuation
have been modernized. Latin and Greek quotations have
been corrected in accordance with the Loeb Classical Library, from which the translations in the notes are taken
unless otherwise stated. Quotations from Milton have been
corrected in accordance with a copy of the second edition of
Paradise Lost (1674) now in the Huntington Library, except

that spelling and punctuation have been modernized. As far as possible all quotations from other English authors have been corrected in accordance with early or standard editions, again with modernization of spelling and punctuation. Since emphasis here is on the immediate impact of Addison's critical essays, notably on the responses to them evoked from the other leading critic of the day, John Dennis, the original texts of the essays are given rather than those of one of the subsequent collected editions, which include, along with non-authorial changes, some revisions by Addison.

For an admirable account of the textual history of *The Spectator*, the reader can consult the edition in five volumes prepared by Donald F. Bond (Clarendon Press, 1965).

I gratefully acknowledge several obligations incurred in editing this book: to the Harvard University Press for permission to quote from the Loeb Classical Library; to the Huntington Library for permission to use the copy texts; to Mrs. Carol B. Pearson, Mr. Jerry Dibble, and Mrs. Joan Bennett for assistance in preparing the text and explanatory notes; to Professors Lillian and Edward Bloom and W. B. Carnochan for valuable criticism of my introduction; and to the late Professor Asher Hinds, who many years ago aroused my interest in the literary theory of the eighteenth century. Insofar as this little book is mine to dedicate, I address it to the memory of Professor Hinds.

PRINCIPAL DATES IN THE LIFE OF JOSEPH ADDISON

1672   Joseph Addison is born in Milston, Wiltshire, May 1, the oldest son of Lancelot Addison, rector of Milston. Richard Steele is also born in this year in Dublin.

1683   Addison's father becomes Dean of Lichfield Cathedral.

1686-1687   Attends the Charterhouse in London, where he makes the acquaintance of Steele.

1687-1689   Undergraduate at Queens' College, Oxford.

1689-1691   Undergraduate at Magdalen College, Oxford.

1691   Bachelor of Arts from Oxford.

1691-1698   Tutor at Oxford.

1693   Master of Arts from Oxford.

1697   Probationary fellow of Magdalen College.

1698-1711   Fellow of Magdalen College.

1699-1703   Travels on the Continent with a pension from the Crown.

1705   *Remarks on Several Parts of Italy* published. "The Campaign," a poem celebrating the Battle of Blenheim, wins him increased influence with the Whigs.

1706-1708   Undersecretary of State.

1707   *Rosamond* (opera with libretto by Addison) performed at Drury Lane in March without success.

1708-1710   Secretary to the Lord Lieutenant of Ireland.

1708-1719   Member of Parliament.

1709-1711   Contributes to Steele's *The Tatler*.

1711-1712   Conducts *The Spectator* in partnership with Steele.

1713   *Cato* performed at Drury Lane in April with immense success. Contributes to Steele's *The Guardian*.

1714   Revives *The Spectator* independently, June to December.

1714   Secretary to the Lords Justices.

1715-1716   Conducts *The Freeholder* in defense of the Hanoverian succession against the Jacobites.

1716   *The Drummer* performed at Drury Lane in March without acknowledgment of Addison's authorship. In August marries the widowed Countess of Warwick.

1717-1718   Secretary of State.

1718   Retires from political life.

1719   Dies June 17. Buried in Westminster Abbey.

HUMOR

No. 35

[False humor and true humor]

Tuesday, April 10, 1711

. . . risu inepto res ineptior nullast.—Mart.[1]

Among all kinds of writing there is none in which authors are more apt to miscarry than in works of humor, as there is none in which they are more ambitious to excel. It is not an imagination that teems with monsters, a head that is filled with extravagant conceptions, which is capable of furnishing the world with diversions of this nature, and yet if we look into the productions of several writers who set up for men of humor, what wild irregular fancies, what unnatural distortions of thought do we meet with? If they speak nonsense, they believe they are talking humor, and when they have drawn together a scheme of absurd inconsistent ideas, they are not able to read it over to themselves without laughing. These poor gentlemen endeavor to gain themselves the reputation of wits and humorists by such monstrous conceits as almost qualify them for Bedlam, not considering that humor should always lie under the check of reason, and that it requires the direction of the nicest judgment by so much the more as it indulges itself in the most

---

1 risu . . . nullast Catullus *Carmina* 39.16: "There is nothing more silly than a silly laugh." (In the first edition this was erroneously attributed to Martial.)

boundless freedoms. There is a kind of nature that is to be observed in this sort of compositions as well as in all other and a certain regularity of thought that must discover the writer to be a man of sense at the same time that he appears altogether given up to caprice. For my part, when I read the delirious mirth of an unskillful author, I cannot be so barbarous as to divert myself with it but am rather apt to pity the man than to laugh at anything he writes.

The deceased Mr. Shadwell,[2] who had himself a great deal of the talent which I am treating of, represents an empty rake in one of his plays as very much surprised to hear one say that breaking of windows was not humor. And I question not but several English readers will be as much startled to hear me affirm that many of those raving incoherent pieces which are often spread among us under odd chimerical titles are rather the offsprings of a distempered brain than works of humor.

It is indeed much easier to describe what is not humor than what is, and very difficult to define it otherwise than as Cowley[3] has done wit, by negatives. Were I to give my own notions of it, I would deliver them after Plato's manner in a kind of allegory and by supposing humor to be a person deduce to him all his qualifications according to the following genealogy. Truth was the founder of the family and the Father of Good Sense. Good Sense was the father of Wit, who married a lady of a collateral line called Mirth by whom he had issue Humor. Humor therefore, being the youngest of the illustrious family and descended from parents of such different dispositions, is very various and unequal in his temper. Sometimes you see him putting on grave looks and a solemn habit, sometimes airy in his behavior and fantastic in his dress, insomuch that at different times he appears as serious as a judge and as jocular as a merry-andrew. But as he has a great deal of the mother in his constitution, whatever mood he is in he never fails to make his company laugh.

But since there are several impostors abroad who take upon them the name of this young gentleman and would willingly pass for him in the world, to the end that well-

2 Mr. Shadwell Thomas Shadwell (1642?-1692) **3 Cowley** Abraham Cowley (1618-1667)

meaning persons may not be imposed upon by counterfeits, I would desire my readers, when they meet with any of these pretenders, to look into his parentage and to examine him strictly whether or no he be remotely allied to Truth, and lineally descended from Good Sense. If not, they may conclude him a counterfeit. They may likewise distinguish him by a loud and excessive laughter, in which he seldom gets his company to join with him. For as True Humor generally looks serious whilst everybody laughs that is about him, False Humor is always laughing whilst everybody about him looks serious. I shall only add, if he has not in him a mixture of both parents, that is, if he would pass for the offspring of Wit without Mirth, or Mirth without Wit, you may conclude him to be altogether spurious and a cheat.

The impostor of whom I am speaking descends originally from Falsehood, who was the mother of Nonsense, who was brought to bed of a son called Frenzy, who married one of the daughters of Folly commonly known by the name of Laughter, on whom he begot that monstrous infant of which I have been here speaking. I shall set down at length the genealogical table of False Humor and at the same time place under it the genealogy of True Humor, that the reader may at one view behold their different pedigrees and relations.

FALSEHOOD
NONSENSE
FRENZY————LAUGHTER
FALSE HUMOR

TRUTH
GOOD SENSE
WIT————MIRTH
HUMOR

I might extend the allegory by mentioning several of the children of False Humor, who are more in number than the sands of the sea, and might in particular enumerate the many sons and daughters which he has begot in this island. But as this would be a very invidious task, I shall only observe in general that False Humor differs from the True as a monkey does from a man.

First of all, he is exceedingly given to little apish tricks and buffooneries.

Secondly, he so much delights in mimicry that it is all one to him whether he exposes by it vice and folly, luxury and avarice, or, on the contrary, virtue and wisdom, pain and poverty.

Thirdly, he is wonderfully unlucky insomuch that he will bite the hand that feeds him and endeavor to ridicule both friends and foes indifferently; for having but small talents he must be merry where he can, not where he should.

Fourthly, being entirely void of reason, he pursues no point either of morality or instruction but is ludicrous only for the sake of being so.

Fifthly, being incapable of having anything but mock-representations, his ridicule is always personal and aimed at the vicious man or the writer, not at the vice or at the writing.

I have here only pointed at the whole species of false humorists, but as one of my principal designs in this paper is to beat down that malignant spirit which discovers itself in the writings of the present age, I shall not scruple for the future to single out any of the small wits that infest the world with such compositions as are ill-natured, immoral, and absurd. This is the only exception which I shall make to the general rule I have prescribed myself of attacking multitudes, since every honest man ought to look upon himself as in a natural state of war with the libeler and lampooner and to annoy them wherever they fall in his way. This is but retaliating upon them and treating them as they treat others.

No. 47

[The psychology of humor]

Tuesday, April 24, 1711

Ride si sapis . . .—Mart.[1]

Mr. Hobbes, in his discourse of *Human Nature*,[2] which in my humble opinion is much the best of all his works, after some very curious observations upon laughter, concludes thus: "The passion of laughter is nothing else but sudden glory arising from some sudden conception of some eminency in ourselves by comparison with the infirmity of others or with our own formerly; for men laugh at the follies of themselves past when they come suddenly to remembrance, except they bring with them any present dishonor."

According to this author, therefore, when we hear a man laugh excessively, instead of saying he is very merry, we ought to tell him he is very proud. And indeed, if we look into the bottom of this matter, we shall meet with many observations to confirm us in his opinion. Everyone laughs at somebody that is in an inferior state of folly to himself. It was formerly the custom for every great house in England to keep a tame fool dressed in petticoats, that the heir of the family might have an opportunity of joking upon him and divert himself with his absurdities. For the same reason idiots are still in request in most of the courts of Germany, where there is not a prince of any great magnificence who

1 Ride . . . sapis Martial *Epigrams* 2.41.1: "Laugh, if you are wise" **2 Mr. Hobbes . . . Human Nature** Thomas Hobbes (1588-1679), *Human Nature, or the Fundamental Elements of Policy* (1650), ix, 13

has not two or three dressed, distinguished, undisputed fools in his retinue whom the rest of the courtiers are always breaking their jests upon.

The Dutch, who are more famous for their industry and application than for wit and humor, hang up in several of their streets what they call the sign of the gaper, that is, the head of an idiot dressed in a cap and bells and gaping in a most immoderate manner. This is a standing jest at Amsterdam.

Thus everyone diverts himself with some person or other that is below him in point of understanding and triumphs in the superiority of his genius whilst he has such objects of derision before his eyes. Mr. Dennis[3] has very well expressed this in a couple of humorous lines, which are a part of a translation of a satire in Monsieur Boileau.[4]

> Thus one fool lolls his tongue out at another,
> And shakes his empty noddle at his brother.

Mr. Hobbes's reflection gives us the reason why the insignificant people above mentioned are stirrers up of laughter among men of a gross taste; but as the more understanding part of mankind do not find their risibility affected by such ordinary objects, it may be worth the while to examine into the several provocatives of laughter in men of superior sense and knowledge.

In the first place I must observe that there is a set of merry drolls whom the common people of all countries admire and seem to love so well that they could eat them, according to the old proverb; I mean those circumforaneous[5] wits whom every nation calls by the name of that dish of meat which it loves best. In Holland they are termed pickled herrings; in France, jean pottages; in Italy, maccaronies; and in Great Britain, jack puddings. These merry wags, from whatsoever food they receive their titles, that they may make their audiences laugh, always appear in a fool's coat and commit

3 Mr. Dennis John Dennis (1657-1734), published in his *Miscellanies in Verse and Prose* (1681). See *Critical Works of John Dennis*, ed. Edward Niles Hooker (Baltimore, 1939,1943), II, 442   **4 Monsieur Boileau** Nicolas Boileau-Despréaux (1636-1711), *Satire* IV   **5 circumforaneous** strolling from market to market; wandering (*OED*)

such blunders and mistakes in every step they take and every word they utter as those who listen to them would be ashamed of.

But this little triumph of the understanding, under the disguise of laughter, is nowhere more visible than in that custom which prevails everywhere among us on the first day of the present month, when everybody takes it in his head to make as many fools as he can. In proportion as there are more follies discovered, so there is more laughter raised on this day than on any other in the whole year. A neighbor of mine, who is a haberdasher by trade and a very shallow conceited fellow, makes his boasts that for these ten years successively he has not made less than a hundred April fools. My landlady had a falling out with him about a fortnight ago for sending every one of her children upon some sleeveless errand, as she terms it. Her eldest son went to buy a halfpennyworth of inkle at a shoemaker's; the eldest daughter was dispatched half a mile to see a monster; and in short the whole family of innocent children made April fools. Nay, my landlady herself did not escape him. This empty fellow has laughed upon these conceits ever since.

This art of wit is well enough when confined to one day in a twelvemonth, but there is an ingenious tribe of men sprung up of late years who are for making April fools every day in the year. These gentlemen are commonly distinguished by the name of biters,[6] a race of men that are perpetually employed in laughing at those mistakes which are of their own production.

Thus we see, in proportion as one man is more refined than another, he chooses his fool out of a lower or higher class of mankind; or, to speak in a more philosophical language, that secret elation and pride of heart which is generally called laughter arises in him from his comparing himself with an object below him, whether it so happens that it be a natural or an artificial fool. It is indeed very possible that the persons we laugh at may in the main of their characters be much wiser men than ourselves, but if they

6 biters Steele defines "biter" (*Tatler*, no. 12) as "a dull fellow that tells you a lie with a grave face, and laughs at you for knowing him no better than to believe him" (Aitken ed., I, 109)

would have us laugh at them they must fall short of us in those respects which stir up this passion.

I am afraid I shall appear too abstracted in my speculations if I show that when a man of wit makes us laugh it is by betraying some oddness or infirmity in his own character or in the representation which he makes of others, and that when we laugh at a brute or even an inanimate thing it is at some action or incident that bears a remote analogy to any blunder or absurdity in reasonable creatures.

But to come into common life, I shall pass by the consideration of those stage coxcombs that are able to shake a whole audience and take notice of a particular sort of men who are such provokers of mirth in conversation that it is impossible for a club or merry meeting to subsist without them. I mean those honest gentlemen that are always exposed to the wit and raillery of their well-wishers and companions, that are pelted by men, women, and children, friends and foes, and, in a word, stand as butts in conversation for everyone to shoot at that pleases. I know several of these butts who are men of wit and sense, though by some odd turn of humor, some unlucky cast in their person or behavior, they have always the misfortune to make the company merry. The truth of it is, a man is not qualified for a butt who has not a good deal of wit and vivacity, even in the ridiculous side of his character. A stupid butt is only fit for the conversation of ordinary people; men of wit require one that will give them play and bestir himself in the absurd part of his behavior. A butt with these accomplishments frequently gets the laugh of his side and turns the ridicule upon him that attacks him. Sir John Falstaff[7] was a hero of this species and gives a good description of himself in his capacity of a butt, after the following manner: "Men of all sorts," says that merry knight, "take a pride to gird at me. The brain of man . . . is not able to invent anything that tends to laughter more than I invent or is invented on me. I am not only witty in myself but the cause that wit is in other men."

C

7 **Sir John Falstaff**   *2 Henry IV*, I. ii. 6

No. 249

[Uses and abuses of ridicule]

Saturday, December 15, 1711

Γέλως ἄκαιρος ἐν βροτοῖς δεινὸν κακόν.—Frag. Vet. Po.[1]

When I make choice of a subject that has not been treated of by others, I throw together my reflections on it without any order or method so that they may appear rather in the looseness and freedom of an essay than in the regularity of a set discourse. It is after this manner that I shall consider laughter and ridicule in my present paper.

Man is the merriest species of the creation; all above and below him are serious. He sees things in a different light from other beings and finds his mirth rising from objects that perhaps cause something like pity or displeasure in higher natures. Laughter is indeed a very good counterpoise to the spleen, and it seems but reasonable that we should be capable of receiving joy from what is no real good to us, since we can receive grief from what is no real evil.

I have in my forty-seventh paper raised a speculation on the notion of a modern philosopher[2] who describes the first motive of laughter to be a secret comparison which we make between ourselves and the persons we laugh at; or, in other words, that satisfaction which we receive from the opinion of some preeminence in ourselves when we see the absurdities of another or when we reflect on any past absurdities

---

1 *Menandri Sententiae*, ed. S. Jackel (Teubner, Leipzig, 1964), 144: "Ill-timed laughter is a grave evil among mortals"   **2 a modern philosopher** Thomas Hobbes

of our own. This seems to hold in most cases, and we may observe that the vainest part of mankind are the most addicted to this passion.

I have read a sermon of a conventual[3] in the Church of Rome on those words of the wise man,[4] "I said of laughter, it is mad, and of mirth, what doeth it?"—upon which he laid it down as a point of doctrine that laughter was the effect of original sin and that Adam could not laugh before the fall.

Laughter, while it lasts, slackens and unbraces the mind, weakens the faculties, and causes a kind of remissness and dissolution in all the powers of the soul, and thus far it may be looked upon as a weakness in the composition of human nature. But if we consider the frequent reliefs that we receive from it and how often it breaks the gloom which is apt to depress the mind and damp our spirits with transient, unexpected gleams of joy, one would take care not to grow too wise for so great a pleasure of life.

The talent of turning men into ridicule and exposing to laughter those one converses with is the qualification of little, ungenerous tempers. A young man with this cast of mind cuts himself off from all manner of improvement. Everyone has his flaws and weaknesses; nay, the greatest blemishes are often found in the most shining characters. But what an absurd thing it is to pass over all the valuable parts of a man and fix our attention on his infirmities, to observe his imperfections more than his virtues, and to make use of him for the sport of others rather than for our own improvement.

We therefore very often find that persons the most accomplished in ridicule are those who are very shrewd at hitting a blot without exerting anything masterly in themselves. As there are many eminent critics who never wrote a good line, there are many admirable buffoons that animadvert upon every single defect in another without ever discovering the least beauty of their own. By this means these unlucky little wits often gain reputation in the esteem of vulgar minds and raise themselves above persons of much more laudable characters.

If the talent of ridicule were employed to laugh men out of

---

3 conventual member of a religious convent   **4 words of the wise man** Ecclesiastes 2:2

vice and folly, it might be of some use to the world; but instead of this, we find that it is generally made use of to laugh men out of virtue and good sense by attacking everything that is solemn and serious, decent and praiseworthy in human life.

We may observe that in the first ages of the world, when the great souls and masterpieces of human nature were produced, men shined by a noble simplicity of behavior and were strangers to those little embellishments which are so fashionable in our present conversation. And it is very remarkable that notwithstanding we fall short at present of the ancients in poetry, painting, oratory, history, architecture, and all the noble arts and sciences which depend more upon genius than experience; we exceed them as much in doggerel, humor, burlesque, and all the trivial arts of ridicule. We meet with more raillery among the moderns, but more good sense among the ancients.

The two great branches of ridicule in writing are comedy and burlesque. The first ridicules persons by drawing them in their proper characters, the other by drawing them quite unlike themselves. Burlesque is therefore of two kinds: the first represents mean persons in the accouterments of heroes; the other describes great persons acting and speaking like the basest among the people. Don Quixote is an instance of the first and Lucian's gods of the second. It is a dispute among the critics whether burlesque poetry runs best in heroic verse, like that of *The Dispensary*,[5] or in doggerel, like that of *Hudibras*.[6] I think that where the low character is to be raised, the heroic is the proper measure, but when a hero is to be pulled down and degraded, it is done best in doggerel.

If Hudibras had been set out with as much wit and humor in heroic verse as he is in doggerel, he would have made a much more agreeable figure than he does, though the generality of his readers are so wonderfully pleased with the double rhymes that I do not expect many will be of my opinion in this particular.

I shall conclude this essay upon laughter with observing that the metaphor of laughing applied to fields and meadows

5 **The Dispensary** (1699), by Sir Samuel Garth (1661-1719)
6 **Hudibras** (1663, 1664, 1678), by Samuel Butler (1612-1680)

when they are in flower or to trees when they are in blossom runs through all languages, which I have not observed of any other metaphor, excepting that of fire and burning when they are applied to love. This shows that we naturally regard laughter as what is in itself both amiable and beautiful. For this reason likewise Venus has gained the title of the laughter-loving dame, as Waller[7] has translated it, and is represented by Horace[8] as the goddess who delights in laughter. Milton,[9] in a joyous assembly of imaginary persons, has given us a very poetical figure of laughter. His whole band of mirth is so finely described that I shall set down the passage at length.

> But come thou Goddess fair and free,
> In heav'n yclept Euphrosyne,
> And by men, heart-easing Mirth,
> Whom lovely Venus at a birth
> With two sister graces more
> To ivy-crowned Bacchus bore:
> . . . .
> Haste thee Nymph, and bring with thee
> Jest and youthful jollity,
> Quips and cranks, and wanton wiles,
> Nods, and becks, and wreathed smiles,
> Such as hang on Hebe's cheek,
> And love to live in dimple sleek;
> Sport that wrinkled Care derides,
> And Laughter holding both his sides.
> Come, and trip it as ye go
> On the light fantastic toe,
> And in thy right hand lead with thee,
> The mountain nymph, sweet Liberty;
> And if I give thee honor due,
> Mirth, admit me of thy crew
> To live with her, and live with thee,
> In unreproved pleasures free.

7 **Waller** Edmund Waller (1606-1687), *The Countess of Carlisle in Mourning*, l. 13 8 **Horace** *Odes* 1.33; 2.8 9 **Milton** *L'Allegro*, ll. 11-16, 25-40

TRAGEDY

No. 39

[The language of tragedy]

Saturday, April 14, 1711

multa fero, ut placem genus irritabile vatum,
cum scribo . . .—Hor.[1]

As a perfect tragedy is the noblest production of human
nature, so it is capable of giving the mind one of the most
delightful and most improving entertainments. A virtuous
man (says Seneca[2]) struggling with misfortunes is such a
spectacle as gods might look upon with pleasure, and such a
pleasure it is which one meets with in the representation of
a well-written tragedy. Diversions of this kind wear out of
our thoughts everything that is mean and little. They
cherish and cultivate that humanity which is the ornament
of our nature. They soften insolence, soothe affliction, and
subdue the mind to the dispensations of Providence.

It is no wonder therefore that in all the polite nations of
the world this part of the drama has met with public encouragement.

The modern tragedy excels that of Greece and Rome in the
intricacy and disposition of the fable, but, what a Christian
writer would be ashamed to own, falls infinitely short of it
in the moral part of the performance.

This I shall show more at large hereafter, and in the
meantime, that I may contribute something towards the
improvement of the English tragedy, I shall take notice, in

1 multa fero . . . scribo Horace *Epistles* 2.2.102: "Much do I endure,
to soothe the fretful tribe of bards, so long as I am scribbling"
2 Seneca *De Providentia* 2

30

this and in other following papers, of some particular parts in it that seem liable to exception.

Aristotle observes[3] that the iambic verse in the Greek tongue was the most proper for tragedy because at the same time that it lifted up the discourse from prose it was that which approached nearer to it than any other kind of verse; for, says he, we may observe that men in ordinary discourse very often speak iambics without taking notice of it. We may make the same observation of our English blank verse which often enters into our common discourse though we do not attend to it and is such a due medium between rhyme and prose that it seems wonderfully adapted to tragedy. I am therefore very much offended when I see a play in rhyme, which is as absurd in English as a tragedy of hexameters would have been in Greek or Latin. The solecism is, I think, still greater in those plays that have some scenes in rhyme and some in blank verse, which are to be looked upon as two several languages, or where we see some particular similes dignified with rhyme at the same time that everything about them lies in blank verse. I would not however debar the poet from concluding his tragedy, or, if he pleases, every act of it, with two or three couplets, which may have the same effect as an air in the Italian opera after a long *recitativo* and give the actor a graceful exit. Besides that, we see a diversity of numbers in some parts of the old tragedy in order to hinder the ear from being tired with the same continued modulation of voice. For the same reason I do not dislike the speeches in our English tragedy that close with a hemistich, or half-verse, notwithstanding the person who speaks after it begins a new verse without filling up the preceding one, nor with abrupt pauses and breakings-off in the middle of a verse when they humor any passion that is expressed by it.

Since I am upon this subject, I must observe that our English poets have succeeded much better in the style than in the sentiments of their tragedies. Their language is very often noble and sonorous, but the sense either very trifling or very common. On the contrary, in the ancient tragedies, and indeed in those of Corneille and Racine,[4] though the expressions are very great, it is the thought that bears them

3 Aristotle observes *Poetics* 4 and *Rhetoric* 3.1   **4 Corneille** Pierre Corneille (1606-1684); **Racine** Jean Baptiste Racine (1639-1699)

up and swells them. For my own part, I prefer a noble sentiment that is depressed with homely language infinitely before a vulgar one that is blown up with all the sound and energy of expression. Whether this defect in our tragedies may arise from want of genius, knowledge, or experience in the writers or from their compliance with the vicious taste of their readers, who are better judges of the language than of the sentiments and consequently relish the one more than the other, I cannot determine. But I believe it might rectify the conduct both of the one and of the other if the writer laid down the whole contexture of his dialogue in plain English before he turned it into blank verse and if the reader, after the perusal of a scene, would consider the naked thought of every speech in it when divested of all its tragic ornaments. By this means, without being imposed upon by words, we may judge impartially of the thought and consider whether it be natural or great enough for the person that utters it, whether it deserves to shine in such a blaze of eloquence or show itself in such a variety of lights as are generally made use of by the writers of our English tragedy.

I must in the next place observe that when our thoughts are great and just they are often obscured by the sounding phrases, hard metaphors, and forced expressions in which they are clothed. Shakespeare is often very faulty in this particular. There is a fine observation in Aristotle to this purpose, which I have never seen quoted. The expression, says he, ought to be very much labored in the unactive parts of the fable, as in descriptions, similitudes, narrations, and the like, in which the opinions, manners, and passions of men are not represented; for these (namely the opinions, manners, and passions) are apt to be obscured by pompous phrases and elaborate expressions. Horace, who copied most of his criticisms after Aristotle, seems to have had his eye on the foregoing rule in the following verses:

et tragicus plerumque dolet sermone pedestri
Telephus et Peleus, cum pauper et exsul uterque
Proicit ampullas et sesquipedalia verba,
si curat cor spectantis tetigisse querella.

Tragedians too lay by their state to grieve;
Peleus and Telephus exiled and poor,
Forget their swelling and gigantic words.[5]

Ld. Roscommon.

Among our modern English poets there is none who was better turned for tragedy than Lee,[6] if instead of favoring the impetuosity of his genius he had restrained it and kept it within its proper bounds. His thoughts are wonderfully suited to tragedy but frequently lost in such a cloud of words that it is hard to see the beauty of them. There is an infinite fire in his works but so involved in smoke that it does not appear in half its luster. He frequently succeeds in the passionate parts of the tragedy, but more particularly where he slackens his efforts and eases the style of those epithets and metaphors in which he so much abounds. What can be more natural, more soft, or more passionate than that line in Statira's speech where she describes the charms of Alexander's conversation?

Then he would talk, good gods how he would talk![7]

That unexpected break in the line and turning the description of his manner of talking into an admiration of it is inexpressibly beautiful and wonderfully suited to the fond character of the person that speaks it. There is a simplicity in the words that outshines the utmost pride of expression.

Otway[8] has followed nature in the language of his tragedy and therefore shines in the passionate parts more than any of our English poets. As there is something familiar and domestic in the fable of his tragedy more than in those of any other poet, he has little pomp but great force in his expressions. For which reason, though he has admirably succeeded in the tender and melting part of his tragedies, he sometimes falls into too great a familiarity of phrase in those parts which, by Aristotle's rule, ought to have been raised and supported by the dignity of expression.

---

5 et tragicus . . . querella Horace *Ars Poetica* 95-8, trans. Wentworth Dillon, fourth Earl of Roscommon (London, 1680) **6 Lee** Nathaniel Lee (ca. 1648-1692) **7 Then he would . . . talk** *The Rival Queens* (1677), I.i: "Then he will talk, good Gods how he will talk!" **8 Otway** Thomas Otway (1652-1685)

It has been observed by others that this poet has founded his tragedy of *Venice Preserved* on so wrong a plot that the greatest characters in it are those of rebels and traitors. Had the hero of his play discovered the same good qualities in the defense of his country that he showed for its ruin and subversion, the audience could not enough pity and admire him; but as he is now represented we can only say of him what the Roman historian[9] says of Catiline, that his fall would have been glorious *(si pro patria sic concidisset)* had he so fallen in the service of his country.

C

No. 40

[Objections to "poetical justice" in tragedy]

Monday, April 16, 1711

> *ac ne forte putes me, quae facere ipse recusem,*
> *cum recte tractent alii, laudare maligne,*
> *ille per extentum funem mihi posse videtur ire poeta,*
> *meum qui pectus inaniter angit,*
> *irritat, mulcet, falsis terroribus implet,*
> *ut magus, et modo me Thebis, modo ponit Athenis.*
> —Hor.[1]

The English writers of tragedy are possessed with a notion that when they represent a virtuous or innocent person in

---

9 the Roman historian Lucius Annaeus Florus, *Epitomae de Tito Livio Bellorum Omnium Annorum DCC* 2.12.12

1 ac ne forte . . . Athenis Horace *Epistles* 2.1.208-13: "And lest, perchance, you may think that I begrudge praise when others are handling well what I decline to try myself, methinks that poet is able to walk a tight rope, who with airy nothings wrings my heart, inflames, soothes, fills it with vain alarms like a magician, and sets me down now at Thebes, now at Athens"

distress they ought not to leave him till they have delivered him out of his troubles or made him triumph over his enemies. This error they have been led into by a ridiculous doctrine in modern criticism, that they are obliged to an equal distribution of rewards and punishments and an impartial execution of poetical justice. Who were the first that established this rule I know not, but I am sure it has no foundation in nature, in reason, or in the practice of the ancients. We find that good and evil happen alike to all men on this side the grave, and, as the principal design of tragedy is to raise commiseration and terror in the minds of the audience, we shall defeat this great end if we always make virtue and innocence happy and successful. Whatever crosses and disappointments a good man suffers in the body of the tragedy, they will make but small impression on our minds when we know that in the last act he is to arrive at the end of his wishes and desires. When we see him engaged in the depth of his afflictions, we are apt to comfort ourselves because we are sure he will find his way out of them and that his grief, how great soever it may be at present, will soon terminate in gladness. For this reason, the ancient writers of tragedy treated men in their plays as they are dealt with in the world by making virtue sometimes happy and sometimes miserable as they found it in the fable which they made choice of or as it might affect their audience in the most agreeable manner. Aristotle considers[2] the tragedies that were written in either of these kinds and observes that those which ended unhappily had always pleased the people and carried away the prize in the public disputes of the stage from those that ended happily. Terror and commiseration leave a pleasing anguish in the mind and fix the audience in such a serious composure of thought as is much more lasting and delightful than any little transient starts of joy and satisfaction. Accordingly we find that more of our English tragedies have succeeded in which the favorites of the audience sink under their calamities than those in which they recover themselves out of them. The best plays of this kind are *The Orphan, Venice Preserved, Alexander the Great, Theodosius, All for Love, Oedipus,*

2 Aristotle considers *Poetics* 31

Oroonoko,[3] *Othello*, etc. *King Lear* is an admirable tragedy of the same kind as Shakespeare wrote it, but as it is reformed[4] according to the chimerical notion of poetical justice, in my humble opinion it has lost half its beauty. At the same time I must allow that there are very noble tragedies which have been framed upon the other plan and have ended happily, as indeed most of the good tragedies which have been written since the starting of the above-mentioned criticism have taken this turn; as *The Mourning Bride, Tamerlane, Ulysses, Phaedra and Hippolitus*,[5] with most of Mr. Dryden's. I must also allow that many of Shakespeare's and several of the celebrated tragedies of antiquity are cast in the same form. I do not therefore dispute against this way of writing tragedies but against the criticism that would establish this as the only method and by that means would very much cramp the English tragedy and perhaps give a wrong bent to the genius of our writers.

The tragicomedy, which is the product of the English theater, is one of the most monstrous inventions that ever entered into a poet's thoughts. An author might as well think of weaving the adventures of Aeneas and Hudibras into one poem as of writing such a motley piece of mirth and sorrow. But the absurdity of these performances is so very visible that I shall not insist upon it.

The same objections which are made to tragicomedy may in some measure be applied to all tragedies that have a double plot in them, which are likewise more frequent upon the English stage than upon any other; for though the grief of the audience in such performances be not changed into another passion, as in tragicomedies, it is diverted upon another object, which weakens their concern for the principal action and breaks the tide of sorrow by throwing it into different channels. This inconvenience, however, may in a

3 **The Orphan** (1680) and **Venice Preserved** (1682) by Thomas Otway; **Alexander the Great** (1677) and **Theodosius** (1680) by Nathaniel Lee; **All for Love** (1678) by John Dryden; **Oedipus** (1679) by Dryden and Lee; **Oroonoko** (1696) by Thomas Southerne 4 **King Lear . . . as it is reformed** by Nahum Tate (1681) 5 **The Mourning Bride** (1697) by William Congreve; **Tamerlane** (1702) and **Ulysses** (1706) by Nicholas Rowe; **Phaedra and Hippolitus** (1707) by Edmund Smith

great measure be cured, if not wholly removed, by the skillful choice of an underplot which may bear such a near relation to the principal design as to contribute towards the completion of it and be concluded by the same catastrophe.

There is also another particular which may be reckoned among the blemishes, or rather the false beauties, of our English tragedy; I mean those particular speeches which are commonly known by the name of rants. The warm and passionate parts of a tragedy are always the most taking with the audience; for which reason we often see the players pronouncing in all the violence of action several parts of the tragedy which the author writ with great temper and designed that they should have been so acted. I have seen Powell[6] very often raise himself a loud clap by this artifice. The poets that were acquainted with this secret have given frequent occasion for such emotions in the actor by adding vehemence to words where there was no passion or inflaming a real passion into fustian. This hath filled the mouths of our heroes with bombast and given them such sentiments as proceed rather from a swelling than a greatness of mind. Unnatural exclamations, curses, vows, blasphemies, a defiance of mankind, and an outraging of the gods frequently pass upon the audience for towering thoughts and have accordingly met with infinite applause.

I shall here add a remark which I am afraid our tragic writers may make an ill use of. As our heroes are generally lovers, their swelling and blustering upon the stage very much recommends them to the fair part of their audience. The ladies are wonderfully pleased to see a man insulting kings or affronting the gods in one scene and throwing himself at the feet of his mistress in another. Let him behave himself insolently towards the men and abjectly towards the fair one, and it is ten to one but he proves a favorite of the boxes. Dryden and Lee in several of their tragedies have practiced this secret with good success.

But to show how a rant pleases beyond the most just and natural thought that is not pronounced with vehemence, I would desire the reader, when he sees the tragedy of *Oedipus*, to observe how quietly the hero is dismissed at the end of the third act after having pronounced the following

6 **Powell** George Powell (1668-1714)

lines, in which the thought is very natural and apt to move
compassion:

> To you, good gods, I make my last appeal;
> Or clear my virtue, or my crimes reveal:
> If wandering in the maze of Fate I run,
> And backward trod the paths I sought to shun,
> Impute my errors to your own decree;
> My hands are guilty, but my heart is free.

Let us then observe with what thunderclaps of applause he
leaves the stage after the impieties and execrations at the
end of the fourth act, and you will wonder to see an audience so cursed and so pleased at the same time.

> O that as oft I have at Athens seen
>   [Where, by the way, there was no stage till
>   many years after *Oedipus*]
> The stage arise, and the big clouds descend;
> So now, in very deed I might behold
> The pond'rous earth, and all yon marble roof
> Meet, like the hand of Jove, and crush mankind!
> For all the elements, etc.[7]

ADVERTISEMENT.

Having spoken of Mr. Powell as sometimes raising himself applause from the ill taste of an audience, I must do him
the justice to own that he is excellently formed for a trage-
dian and, when he pleases, deserves the admiration of the
best judges, as I doubt not but he will in the *Conquest of
Mexico*,[8] which is acted for his own benefit tomorrow night.

                                                              C

---

7 **To you, good gods . . . elements** *Oedipus* III.i; IV.i
8 **Conquest of Mexico** Dryden's *The Indian Emperor* (1665)

No. 42

[The staging of tragedy]

Wednesday, April 18, 1711

> *Garganum mugire putes nemus aut mare Tuscum;*
> *tanto cum strepitu ludi spectantur et artes*
> *divitiaeque peregrinae, quibus oblitus actor*
> *cum stetit in scaena, concurrit dextera laevae.*
> *"dixit adhuc aliquid?" "nil sane." "quid placet ergo?"*
> *"lana Tarentino violas imitata veneno."*—Hor.[1]

Aristotle[2] has observed that ordinary writers in tragedy endeavor to raise terror and pity in their audience not by proper sentiments and expressions but by the dresses and decorations of the stage. There is something of this kind very ridiculous in the English theater. When the author has a mind to terrify us, it thunders; when he would make us melancholy, the stage is darkened. But among all our tragic artifices I am the most offended at those which are made use of to inspire us with magnificent ideas of the persons that speak. The ordinary method of making a hero is to clap a huge plume of feathers upon his head which rises so very high that there is often a greater length from his chin to the

---

1 **Garganum mugire . . . veneno** Horace *Epistles* 2.1.202-7: "One might think it was the roaring of the Garganian forest or of the Tuscan Sea: amid such clamor is the entertainment viewed, the works of art, and the foreign finery, and when, overlaid with this, the actor steps upon the stage, the right hand clashes with the left. 'Has he yet said anything?' Not a word. 'Then what takes them so?' 'Tis the woollen robe that vies with the violet in its Tarentine dye"   2 **Aristotle** *Poetics* 14

top of his head than to the sole of his foot. One would believe that we thought a great man and a tall man the same thing. This very much embarrasses the actor, who is forced to hold his neck extremely stiff and steady all the while he speaks, and notwithstanding any anxieties which he pretends for his mistress, his country, or his friends, one may see by his action that his greatest care and concern is to keep the plume of feathers from falling off his head. For my own part, when I see a man uttering his complaints under such a mountain of feathers, I am apt to look upon him rather as an unfortunate lunatic than a distressed hero. As these superfluous ornaments upon the head make a great man, a princess generally receives her grandeur from those additional encumbrances that fall into her tail; I mean the broad sweeping train that follows her in all her motions and finds constant employment for a boy who stands behind her to open and spread it to advantage. I do not know how others are affected at this sight, but I must confess my eyes are wholly taken up with the page's part; and as for the queen, I am not so attentive to anything she speaks as to the right adjusting of her train, lest it should chance to trip up her heels or incommode her as she walks to and fro upon the stage. It is, in my opinion, a very odd spectacle to see a queen venting her passion in a disordered motion and a little boy taking care all the while that they do not ruffle the tail of her gown. The parts that the two persons act on the stage at the same time are very different: the princess is afraid lest she should incur the displeasure of the king her father or lose the hero her lover, whilst her attendant is only concerned lest she should entangle her feet in her petticoat.

We are told that an ancient tragic poet, to move the pity of his audience for his exiled kings and distressed heroes, used to make the actors represent them in dresses and clothes that were threadbare and decayed. This artifice for moving pity seems as ill contrived as that we have been speaking of to inspire us with a great idea of the persons introduced upon the stage. In short, I would have our conceptions raised by the dignity of thought and sublimity of expression rather than by a train of robes or a plume of feathers.

Another mechanical method of making great men and adding dignity to kings and queens is to accompany them with halberds and battle-axes. Two or three shifters of scenes, with the two candlesnuffers, make up a complete body of guards upon the English stage, and by the addition of a few porters dressed in red coats can represent above a dozen legions. I have sometimes seen a couple of armies drawn up together upon the stage when the poet has been disposed to do honor to his generals. It is impossible for the reader's imagination to multiply twenty men into such prodigious multitudes, or to fancy that two or three hundred thousand soldiers are fighting in a room of forty or fifty yards in compass. Incidents of such nature should be told, not represented.

> . . . non tamen intus
> digna geri promes in scaenam, multaque tolles
> ex oculis, quae mox narret facundia praesens—Hor.[3]

> Yet there are things improper for a scene,
> Which men of judgment only will relate;—L. Roscom.[4]

I should therefore in this particular recommend to my countrymen the example of the French stage, where the kings and queens always appear unattended and leave their guards behind the scenes. I should likewise be glad if we imitated the French in banishing from our stage the noise of drums, trumpets, and huzzas, which is sometimes so very great that when there is a battle in the Haymarket Theater one may hear it as far as Charing Cross.

I have here only touched upon those particulars which are made use of to raise and aggrandize the persons of a tragedy and shall show in another paper the several expedients which are practiced by authors of a vulgar genius to move terror, pity, or admiration in their hearers.

The tailor and the painter often contribute to the success of a tragedy more than the poet. Scenes affect ordinary minds as much as speeches, and our actors are very sensible that a well-dressed play has sometimes brought them as full audiences as a well-written one. The Italians have a very

---

3 non tamen . . . praesens Horace *Ars Poetica* 182-4   **4 L. Roscom**. Wentworth Dillon, fourth Earl of Roscommon (1633-1685)

good phrase to express this art of imposing upon the spectators by appearances. They call it the *fourberia della scena*, the knavery or trickish part of the drama. But however the show and outside of the tragedy may work upon the vulgar, the more understanding part of the audience immediately see through it and despise it.

A good poet will give the reader a more lively idea of an army or a battle in a description than if he actually saw them drawn up in squadrons and battalions or engaged in the confusion of a fight. Our minds should be opened to great conceptions and inflamed with glorious sentiments by what the actor speaks more than by what he appears. Can all the trappings or equipage of a king or hero give Brutus half that pomp and majesty which he receives from a few lines in Shakespeare?

C

No. 44

[The depiction of violence in tragedy]

Friday, April 20, 1711

Tu quid ego et populus mecum desideret audi—Hor.[1]

Among the several artifices which are put in practice by the poets to fill the minds of the audience with terror, the first place is due to thunder and lightning, which are often made use of at the descending of a god, or the rising of a ghost, at the vanishing of a devil, or at the death of a tyrant. I have known a bell introduced into several tragedies with good effect and have seen the whole assembly in a very great alarm all the while it has been ringing. But there is nothing

1 **Tu quid ego . . . audi** Horace *Ars Poetica* 153: "Now hear what I, and with me the public, expect"

which delights and terrifies our English theater so much as a ghost, especially when he appears in a bloody shirt. A specter has very often saved a play though he has done nothing but stalked across the stage or rose through a cleft of it and sunk again without speaking one word. There may be a proper season for these several terrors, and when they only come in as aids and assistances to the poet they are not only to be excused but to be applauded. Thus the sounding of the clock in *Venice Preserved* makes the hearts of the whole audience quake and conveys a stronger terror to the mind than it is possible for words to do. The appearance of the ghost in *Hamlet* is a masterpiece in its kind, and wrought up with all the circumstances that can create either attention or horror. The mind of the reader is wonderfully prepared for his reception by the discourses that precede it; his dumb behavior at his first entrance strikes the imagination very strongly, but every time he enters he is still more terrifying. Who can read the speech with which young Hamlet accosts him, without trembling?

Hor. Look, my Lord, it comes!
Ham. Angels and ministers of grace defend us!
Be thou a spirit of health or goblin damned;
Bring with thee airs from heaven or blasts from hell,
Be thy intents wicked or charitable,
Thou com'st in such a questionable shape
That I will speak to thee. I'll call thee Hamlet,
King, father, royal Dane: O answer me;
Let me not burst in ignorance, but tell
Why thy canonized bones, hearsed in death,
Have burst their cerements; why the sepulcher,
Wherein we saw thee quietly inurned,
Hath op'd his ponderous and marble jaws,
To cast thee up again? What may this mean,
That thou, dead corse, again in complete steel,
Revisits thus the glimpses of the moon,
Making night hideous?[2]

I do not therefore find fault with the artifices above mentioned when they are introduced with skill and accom-

---

2 Hor. Look, my Lord . . . hideous *Hamlet*, I.iv.38-54

panied by proportionable sentiments and expressions in the writing.

For the moving of pity our principal machine is the handkerchief, and indeed in our common tragedies we should not know very often that the persons are in distress by anything they say if they did not from time to time apply their handkerchiefs to their eyes. Far be it from me to think of banishing this instrument of sorrow from the stage; I know a tragedy could not subsist without it. All that I would contend for is to keep it from being misapplied. In a word, I would have the actor's tongue sympathize with his eyes.

A disconsolate mother with a child in her hand has frequently drawn compassion from the audience and has therefore gained a place in several tragedies. A modern writer that observed how this had took in other plays, being resolved to double the distress and melt his audience twice as much as those before him had done, brought a princess upon the stage with a little boy in one hand and a girl in the other. This too had a very good effect. A third poet, being resolved to outwrite all his predecessors, a few years ago introduced three children with great success, and, as I am informed, a young gentleman who is fully determined to break the most obdurate hearts has a tragedy by him where the first person that appears upon the stage is an afflicted widow in her mourning weeds with half a dozen fatherless children attending her, like those that usually hang about the figure of Charity. Thus several incidents that are beautiful in a good writer become ridiculous by falling into the hands of a bad one.

But among all our methods of moving pity or terror there is none so absurd and barbarous and, what more, exposes us to the contempt and ridicule of our neighbors than that dreadful butchering of one another which is so very frequent upon the English stage. To delight in seeing men stabbed, poisoned, racked, or impaled is certainly the sign of a cruel temper. And as this is often practiced before the British audience, several French critics, who think these are grateful spectacles to us, take occasion from them to represent us as a people that delight in blood. It is indeed very odd to see our stage strowed with carcasses in the last scene of a tragedy and to observe in the wardrobe of the playhouse several daggers, poniards, wheels, bowls for poison, and many other instruments of death. Murders and executions are always transacted behind the scenes in the French theater, which in general is very agreeable to the manners of a polite and civilized people. But as there are no exceptions to this rule on the French stage, it leads them into absurdities almost as ridiculous as that which falls under our present censure. I remember in the famous play of Corneille[3] written upon the subject of the Horatii and Curiatii the fierce young hero who had overcome the Curiatii one after another, instead of being congratulated by his sister for his victory, being upbraided by her for having slain her lover, in the height of his passion and resentment kills her. If anything could extenuate so brutal an action it would be the doing of it on a sudden, before the sentiments of nature, reason, or manhood could take place in him. However, to avoid public bloodshed, as soon as his passion is wrought to its height, he follows his sister the whole length of the stage and forbears killing her till they are both withdrawn behind the scenes. I must confess, had he murdered her before the audience, the indecency might have been greater, but as it is, it appears very unnatural and looks like killing in cold blood. To give my opinion upon this case: the fact ought not to have been represented but to have been told if there was any occasion for it.

It may not be unacceptable to the reader to see how Sophocles has conducted a tragedy[4] under the like delicate circumstances. Orestes was in the same condition with Hamlet in Shakespeare, his mother having murdered his father and taken possession of his kingdom in conspiracy with her adulterer. That young prince therefore, being determined to revenge his father's death upon those who filled his throne, conveys himself by a beautiful stratagem into his mother's apartment with a resolution to kill her. But because such a spectacle would have been too shocking to the audience, this dreadful resolution is executed behind the scenes: the mother is heard calling out to her son for mercy, and the son answering her that she showed no mercy to his father. After which she shrieks out that she is wounded, and by what follows we find that she is slain. I don't remember that in any of our plays there are speeches

3 **famous play of Corneille** *Horace* (1640)   4 **Sophocles . . . tragedy** *Electra*

made behind the scenes, though there are other instances of this nature to be met with in those of the ancients. And I believe my reader will agree with me that there is something infinitely more affecting in this dreadful dialogue between the mother and her son behind the scenes than could have been in anything transacted before the audience. Orestes immediately after meets the usurper at the entrance of his palace and, by a very happy thought of the poet, avoids killing him before the audience by telling him that he should live some time in his present bitterness of soul before he would dispatch him, and ordering him to retire into that part of the palace where he had slain his father, whose murder he would revenge in the very same place where it was committed. By this means the poet observes that decency, which Horace afterwards established by a rule, of forbearing to commit parricides or unnatural murders before the audience.

Nec coram populo natos Medea trucidet.[5]

Let not Medea draw her murd'ring knife,
And spill her children's blood upon the stage.

The French have therefore refined too much upon Horace's rule, who never designed to banish all kinds of death from the stage, but only such as had too much horror in them and which would have a better effect upon the audience when transacted behind the scenes. I would therefore recommend to my countrymen the practice of the ancient poets, who were very sparing of their public executions and rather chose to perform them behind the scenes if it could be done with as great an effect upon the audience. At the same time I must observe that though the devoted persons of the tragedy were seldom slain before the audience, which has generally something ridiculous in it, their bodies were often produced after their death, which has always in it something melancholy or terrifying, so that the killing on the stage does not seem to have been avoided only as an indecency but also as an improbability.

5 Nec coram . . . trucidet *Ars Poetica* 185 ff. Here the quoted line is not an accurate rendering of Horace's text. For a faithful version of it, see the next quotation

ne pueros coram populo Medea trucidet,
aut humana palam coquat exta nefarius Atreus,
aut in avem Procne vertatur, Cadmus in anguem.
quodcumque ostendis mihi sic, incredulus odi.—Hor.

Medea must not draw her murdering knife,
Nor Atreus there his horrid feast prepare,
Cadmus's and Progne's metamorphosis
(She to a swallow turned, he to a snake)
And whatsoever contradicts my sense,
I hate to see, and never can believe.—L. Roscom.[6]

I have now gone through the several dramatic inventions
which are made use of by the ignorant poets to supply the
place of tragedy and by skillful ones to improve it, some of
which I could wish entirely rejected and the rest to be used
with caution. It would be an endless task to consider comedy in the same light and to mention the innumerable shifts
that small wits put in practice to raise a laugh. Bullock[7] in a
short coat, and Norris[8] in a long one, seldom fail of this
effect. In ordinary comedies a broad- and a narrow-
brimmed hat are different characters. Sometimes the wit of
the scene lies in a shoulder belt and sometimes in a pair of
whiskers. A lover running about the stage with his head
peeping out of a barrel[9] was thought a very good jest in King
Charles the Second's time and invented by one of the first
wits of that age. But because ridicule is not so delicate as
compassion, and as the objects that make us laugh are infinitely more numerous than those that make us weep, there
is a much greater latitude for comic than tragic artifices and
by consequence a much greater indulgence to be allowed
them.

C

6 L. Roscom. Wentworth Dillon, fourth Earl of Roscommon   7
Bullock William Bullock (ca. 1677-1742)   8 Norris Henry Norris
(1665-1731)   9 A lover . . . barrel in Etherege's *Comical Revenge or
Love in a Tub* (1664)

No. 548

[Objections to "poetical justice" clarified]

Friday, November 28, 1712

> . . . *vitiis nemo sine nascitur: optimus ille est,*
> *qui minimis urgetur.* . . .—Hor.[1]

Mr. Spectator,   Nov. 27, 1712

I have read this day's paper with a great deal of pleasure
and could send you an account of several elixirs and anti-
dotes in your third volume which your correspondents have
not taken notice of in their advertisements, and at the same
time must own to you that I have seldom seen a shop
furnished with such a variety of medicaments and in which
there are fewer soporifics. The several vehicles you have
invented for conveying your unacceptable truths to us are
what I most particularly admire, as I am afraid they are
secrets which will die with you. I do not find that any of
your critical essays are taken notice of in this paper, notwithstanding I look upon them to be excellent cleansers of
the brain and could venture to superscribe them with an
advertisement which I have lately seen in one of our news-
papers, wherein there is an account given of a sovereign
remedy for restoring the taste to all such persons whose
palates have been vitiated by distempers, unwholesome
food, or any the like occasions. But to let fall the allusion,
notwithstanding your criticisms, and particularly the candor which you have discovered in them, are not the least

---

1 vitiis nemo . . . urgetur Horace *Satires* 1.3.68-9: ". . . no living
wight is without faults: the best is he who is burdened with the
least"

taking part of your works, I find your opinion concerning poetical justice as it is expressed in the first part of your fortieth *Spectator* is controverted by some eminent critics;[2] and as you now seem, to our great grief of heart, to be winding up your bottoms,[3] I hoped you would have enlarged a little upon that subject. It is indeed but a single paragraph in your works, and I believe those who have read it with the same attention I have done will think there is nothing to be objected against it. I have, however, drawn up some additional arguments to strengthen the opinion which you have there delivered, having endeavored to go to the bottom of that matter, which you may either publish or suppress as you think fit.

Horace in my motto says that all men are vicious and that they differ from one another only as they are more or less so. Boileau[4] has given the same account of our wisdom as Horace has of our virtue.

Tous les hommes sont fous et, malgré tous leurs soins,
Ne différent entre eux que du plus ou du moins.

All men are fools and, in spite of their endeavors to the contrary, differ from one another only as they are more or less so.

Two or three of the old Greek poets have given the same turn to a sentence which describes the happiness of man in this life:

Τὸ ζῆν ἀλύπως ἀνδρός ἐστιν εὐτυχοῦς.

That man is most happy who is the least miserable.[5]

It will not perhaps be unentertaining to the polite reader to observe how these three beautiful sentences are formed

---

2 some eminent critics presumably a reference to John Dennis. See his reply to *Spectator* no. 40 in his *Original Letters* (1721), pp. 407-16 **3 bottoms** a clew or nucleus on which to wind thread; also skeins, balls of thread (*OED*) **4 Boileau** *Satires* IV, 39-40 **5 Τὸ ζῆν ̄ εὐτυχοῦς.** proverbial, literally "For man, to live without pain is to prosper" (trans. G. de F. Lord)

upon different subjects by the same way of thinking; but I shall return to the first of them.

Our goodness being of a comparative and not an absolute nature, there is none who in strictness can be called a virtuous man. Everyone has in him a natural alloy, though one may be fuller of dross than another. For this reason I cannot think it right to introduce a perfect or a faultless man upon the stage—not only because such a character is improper to move compassion, but because there is no such thing in nature. This might probably be one reason why the Spectator in one of his papers took notice of that late invented term called *poetical justice* and the wrong notions into which it has led some tragic writers. The most perfect man has vices enough to draw down punishments upon his head and to justify Providence in regard to any miseries that may befall him. For this reason I cannot think but that the instruction and moral are much finer where a man who is virtuous in the main of his character falls into distress and sinks under the blows of fortune at the end of a tragedy, than when he is represented as happy and triumphant. Such an example corrects the insolence of human nature, softens the mind of the beholder with sentiments of pity and compassion, comforts him under his own private affliction, and teaches him not to judge of men's virtues by their successes. I cannot think of one real hero in all antiquity so far raised above human infirmities that he might not be very naturally represented in a tragedy as plunged in misfortunes and calamities. The poet may still find out some prevailing passion or indiscretion in his character and show it in such a manner as will sufficiently acquit the gods of any injustice in his sufferings. For, as Horace observes in my text, the best man is faulty, though not in so great a degree as those whom we generally call vicious men.

If such a strict poetical justice as some gentlemen insist upon were to be observed in this art, there is no manner of reason why it should not extend to heroic poetry as well as tragedy. But we find it so little observed in Homer that his Achilles is placed in the greatest point of glory and success, though his character is morally vicious and only poetically good, if I may use the phrase of our modern critics. The *Aeneid* is filled with innocent unhappy persons. Nisus and

Eurialus, Lausus and Pallas[6] come all to unfortunate ends.
The poet takes notice in particular that in the sacking of Troy
Ripheus fell, who was the most just man among the Trojans,

> . . . cadit et Ripheus iustissimus unus
> qui fuit in Teucris et servantissimus aequi
> (dis aliter visum) . . .[7]

and that Pantheus could neither be preserved by his trans-
cendent piety nor by the holy fillets of Apollo, whose priest
he was,

> . . . nec te tua plurima, Panthu,
> labentem pietas nec Apollinis infula texit.
> —Aen. L. 2.[8]

I might here mention the practice of ancient tragic poets,
both Greek and Latin, but as this particular is touched upon
in the paper above mentioned, I shall pass it over in silence.
I could produce passages out of Aristotle in favor of my
opinion, and, if in one place he says that an absolutely
virtuous man should not be represented as unhappy, this
does not justify anyone who shall think fit to bring in an
absolutely virtuous man upon the stage. Those who are
acquainted with that author's way of writing know very
well that, to take the whole extent of his subject into his
divisions of it, he often makes use of such cases as are
imaginary and not reducible to practice. He himself declares
that such tragedies as ended unhappily bore away the prize
in theatrical contentions from those which ended happily;
and for the fortieth speculation, which I am now considering, as it has given reasons why these are more apt to please
an audience, so it only proves that these are generally pref-

6 **Nisus and Eurialus** companions of Aeneas; **Lausus** killed while
fighting with Turnus against Aeneas; **Pallas** companion of Aeneas
who was killed by Turnus 7 **cadit . . . visum** *Aeneid* 2.426-8:
"Ripheus, too, falls, foremost in justice among the Trojans, and
most zealous for the right—Heaven's will was otherwise . . ." 8
nec te . . . texit *Aeneid* 2.429-30: ". . . nor could all thy goodness,
Panthus, nor Apollo's fillet shield thee in thy fall"

erable to the other, though at the same time it affirms that many excellent tragedies have and may be written in both kinds.[9]

---

9 in both kinds In the collected editions, Addison appended the following paragraph: "I shall conclude with observing that though the *Spectator* above mentioned is so far against the rule of poetical justice as to affirm that good men may meet with an unhappy catastrophe in tragedy, it does not say that ill men may go off unpunished. The reason for this distinction is very plain—namely, because the best of men are vicious enough to justify Providence for any misfortunes and afflictions which may befall them, but there are many men so criminal that they can have no claim or pretense to happiness. The best of men may deserve punishment, but the worst of men cannot deserve happiness"

TRUE AND FALSE WIT

No. 58

[Varieties of false wit]

Monday, May 7, 1711

Ut pictura poesis erit . . .—Hor.[1]

Nothing is so much admired and so little understood as wit. No author that I know of has written professedly upon it, and as for those who make any mention of it, they only treat on the subject as it has accidentally fallen in their way, and that too in little short reflections or in general declamatory flourishes, without entering into the bottom of the matter. I hope therefore I shall perform an acceptable work to my countrymen if I treat at large upon this subject, which I shall endeavor to do in a manner suitable to it that I may not incur the censure which a famous critic[2] bestows upon one who had written a treatise upon the sublime in a low groveling style. I intend to lay aside a whole week for this undertaking that the scheme of my thoughts may not be broken and interrupted, and I dare promise myself, if my readers will give me a week's attention, that this great city will be very much changed for the better by next Saturday night. I shall

1 **Ut pictura . . . erit** A poem is like a picture. . . . "Horace's words (*Ars Poetica* 361) are 'Ut pictura poesis: erit . . . ,' but Addison is quoting the opening lines of du Fresnoy's *De Arte Graphica* (1658)" **2 a famous critic** Longinus (d. 273 A.D.)

53

endeavor to make what I say intelligible to ordinary capacities; but if my readers meet with any paper that in some parts of it may be a little out of their reach, I would not have them discouraged, for they may assure themselves the next shall be much clearer.

As the great and only end of these my speculations is to banish vice and ignorance out of the territories of Great Britain, I shall endeavor as much as possible to establish among us a taste of polite writing. It is with this view that I have endeavored to set my readers right in several points relating to operas and tragedies and shall from time to time impart my notions of comedy as I think they may tend to its refinement and perfection. I find by my bookseller that these papers of criticism, with that upon humor, have met with a more kind reception than indeed I could have hoped for from such subjects, for which reason I shall enter upon my present undertaking with greater cheerfulness.

In this and one or two following papers I shall trace out the history of false wit and distinguish the several kinds of it as they have prevailed in different ages of the world. This I think the more necessary at present because I observed there were attempts on foot last winter to revive some of those antiquated modes of wit that have been long exploded out of the commonwealth of letters. There were several satires and panegyrics handed about in acrostic, by which means some of the most arrant, undisputed blockheads about the town began to entertain ambitious thoughts and to set up for polite authors. I shall therefore describe at length those many arts of false wit in which a writer does not show himself a man of beautiful genius but of great industry.

The first species of false wit which I have met with is very venerable for its antiquity and has produced several pieces which have lived very near as long as the *Iliad* itself. I mean those short poems printed among the minor Greek poets[3] which resemble the figure of an egg, a pair of wings, an ax, a shepherd's pipe, and an altar. As for the first, it is a little oval poem and may not improperly be called a scholar's egg. I would endeavor to hatch it or, in more intelligible language, to translate it into English did not I find the interpre-

3 the minor Greek poets For examples of these poems see *Poetae Minores Graeci*, ed. Ralph Winterton (Cambridge, 1635), pp. 349-63

tation of it very difficult; for the author seems to have been more intent upon the figure of his poem than upon the sense of it.

The pair of wings consist of twelve verses, or rather feathers, every verse decreasing gradually in its measure according to its situation in the wing. The subject of it (as in the rest of the poems which follow) bears some remote affinity with the figure, for it describes a god of love, who is always painted with wings.

The ax methinks would have been a good figure for a lampoon had the edge of it consisted of the most satirical parts of the work; but as it is in the original I take it to have been nothing else but the poesy of an ax which was consecrated to Minerva[4] and was thought to have been the same that Epeus made use of in the building of the Trojan horse, which is a hint I shall leave to the consideration of the critics. I am apt to think that the poesy was written originally upon the ax like those which our modern cutlers inscribe upon their knives, and that therefore the poesy still remains in its ancient shape though the ax itself is lost.

The shepherd's pipe may be said to be full of music, for it is composed of nine different kinds of verses that by their several lengths resemble the nine stops of that old musical instrument which is likewise the subject of the poem.

The altar is inscribed with the epitaph of Troilus,[5] the son of Hecuba,[6] which, by the way, makes me believe that these false pieces of wit are much more ancient than the authors to whom they are generally ascribed. At least I will never be persuaded that so fine a writer as Theocritus[7] could have been the author of any such simple works.

It was impossible for a man to succeed in these performances that was not a kind of painter or at least a designer. He was first of all to draw the outline of the subject which he intended to write upon and afterwards conform the description to the figure of his subject. The poetry was to contract or dilate itself according to the mold in which it was cast. In a word, the verses were to be cramped or extended to the dimensions of the frame that was prepared for them and to undergo the fate of those persons whom the tyrant Pro-

4 **Minerva** the Roman goddess of handicraft   5 **Troilus** a son of King Priam of Troy   6 **Hecuba** second wife of King Priam   7 **Theocritus** Greek poet of the third century

crustes used to lodge in his iron bed: if they were too short he stretched them on a rack, and if they were too long chopped off a part of their legs, till they fitted the couch which he had prepared for them.

Mr. Dryden hints at this obsolete kind of wit in one of the following verses which an English reader cannot understand who does not know that there are those little poems above mentioned in the shape of wings and altars.

> . . . choose for thy command,
> Some peaceful province in Acrostic land;
> There may'st thou wings display, and altars raise,
> And torture one poor word a thousand ways[8] . . .

This fashion of false wit was revived by several poets of the last age and in particular may be met with among Mr. Herbert's poems and, if I am not mistaken, in the translation of Du Bartas.[9] I do not remember any other kind of work among the moderns which more resembles the performances I have mentioned than that famous picture of King Charles the First which has the whole Book of Psalms written in the lines of the face and the hair of the head. When I was last at Oxford I perused one of the whiskers and was reading the other, but could not go so far in it as I would have done by reason of the impatience of my friends and fellow travelers, who all of them pressed to see such a piece of curiosity. I have since heard that there is now an eminent writing master in town who has transcribed all the Old Testament in a full-bottomed periwig, and if the fashion should introduce the thick kind of wigs which were in vogue some few years ago he promises to add two or three supernumerary locks that shall contain all the Apocrypha. He designed this wig originally for King William, having disposed of the two Books of Kings in the two forks of the foretop; but that glorious monarch dying before the wig was finished, there is a space left in it for the face of anyone that has a mind to purchase it.

---

8 choose . . . ways Dryden's *Mac Flecknoe*, ll. 205-8   **9 Du Bartas** Guillaume de Salluste Du Bartas' *La Semaine* (1587) was translated by Joshua Sylvester (1605)

But to return to our ancient poems in picture, I would humbly propose for the benefit of our modern smatterers in poetry that they would imitate their brethren among the ancients in those ingenious devices. I have communicated this thought to a young poetical lover of my acquaintance who intends to present his mistress with a copy of verses made in the shape of her fan and, if he tells me true, has already finished the three first sticks of it. He has likewise promised me to get the measure of his mistress's marriage finger with a design to make a poesy in the fashion of a ring which shall exactly fit it. It is so very easy to enlarge upon a good hint that I do not question but my ingenious readers will apply what I have said to many other particulars and that we shall see the town filled in a very little time with poetical tippets,[10] handkerchiefs, snuffboxes, and the like female ornaments. I shall therefore conclude with a word of advice to those admirable English authors who call themselves Pindaric writers, that they would apply themselves to this kind of wit without loss of time as being provided better than any other poets with verses of all sizes and dimensions.

C

No. 59

[Varieties of false wit]

Tuesday, May 8, 1711

. . . *operose nihil agant*. . .—Sen.[1]

There is nothing more certain than that every man would be a wit if he could, and notwithstanding pedants of pretended depth and solidity are apt to decry the writings of a polite

10 **tippet** a cape or short cloak, often with hanging ends (*OED*)
1 **operose . . . agant** Seneca *De Brevitate Vitae* 13.1: ". . . those are laborious triflers . . ."

author as flash and froth, they all of them show upon occasion that they would spare no pains to arrive at the character of those whom they seem to despise. For this reason we often find them endeavoring at works of fancy, which cost them infinite pangs in the production. The truth of it is, a man had better be a galley slave than a wit were one to gain that title by those elaborate trifles which have been the inventions of such authors as were often masters of great learning but no genius.

In my last paper I mentioned some of these false wits among the ancients and in this shall give the reader two or three other species of them that flourished in the same early ages of the world. The first I shall produce are the lipogrammatists or letter-droppers of antiquity that would take an exception, without any reason, against some particular letter in the alphabet so as not to admit it once into a whole poem. One Tryphiodorus[2] was a great master in this kind of writing. He composed an Odyssey or epic poem on the adventures of Ulysses consisting of four and twenty books, having entirely banished the letter *A* from his first book, which was called *Alpha* (as *Lucus a non lucendo*[3]) because there was not an alpha in it. His second book was inscribed *Beta* for the same reason. In short, the poet excluded the whole four and twenty letters in their turns and showed them, one after another, that he could do his business without them.

It must have been very pleasant to have seen this poet avoiding the reprobate letter as much as another would a false quantity and making his escape from it through the several Greek dialects when he was pressed with it in any particular syllable; for the most apt and elegant word in the whole language was rejected like a diamond with a flaw in it if it appeared blemished with a wrong letter. I shall only observe upon this head that if the work I have here mentioned had been now extant, the *Odyssey* of Tryphiodorus in all probability would have been oftener quoted by our

---

2 Tryphiodorus epic poet of the fifth century A.D.   **3 Lucus a non lucendo** folk etymology, "a wood (*lucus*) so-called because there is no light (*lux*) there"

learned pedants than the *Odyssey* of Homer. What a per-petual fund would it have been of obsolete words and phrases, unusual barbarisms and rusticities, absurd spel-lings and complicated dialects? I make no question but it would have been looked upon as one of the most valuable treasuries of the Greek tongue.

I find likewise among the ancients that ingenious kind of conceit which the moderns distinguish by the name of a rebus, that does not sink a letter but a whole word by substituting a picture in its place. When Caesar was one of the masters of the Roman mint, he placed the figure of an elephant upon the reverse of the public money, the word "Caesar" signifying an elephant in the Punic language. This was artificially contrived by Caesar because it was not law-ful for a private man to stamp his own figure upon the coin of the commonwealth. Cicero, who was so called from the founder of his family that was marked on the nose with a little wen like a vetch[4] (which is *cicer* in Latin), instead of Marcus Tullius Cicero ordered the words Marcus Tullius with the figure of a vetch at the end of 'em to be inscribed on a public monument. This was done probably to show that he was neither ashamed of his name or family, notwith-standing the envy of his competitors had often reproached him with both. In the same manner we read of a famous building that was marked in several parts of it with the figures of a frog and a lizard, those words in Greek having been the names of the architects, who by the laws of their country were never permitted to inscribe their own names upon their works. For the same reason it is thought that the forelock of the horse in the antique equestrian statue of Marcus Aurelius represents at a distance the shape of an owl to imitate the country of the statuary, who, in all probabil-ity, was an Athenian. This kind of wit was very much in vogue among our own countrymen about an age or two ago, who did not practice it for any oblique reason as the an-cients above mentioned, but purely for the sake of being witty. Among innumerable instances that may be given of this nature, I shall produce the device of one Mr. Newberry

---

4 **vetch** bean-like fruit (*OED*)

as I find it mentioned by our learned Camden[5] in his *Remains*. Mr. Newberry, to represent his name by a picture, hung up at his door the sign of a yew tree that had several berries upon it, and in the midst of them a great golden N hung upon a bough of the tree, which by the help of a little false spelling made up the word N-ew-berry.

I shall conclude this topic with a rebus[6] which has been lately hewn out in freestone and erected over two of the portals of Blenheim House,[7] being the figure of a monstrous lion tearing to pieces a little cock. For the better understanding of which device I must acquaint my English reader that a cock has the misfortune to be called in Latin by the same word that signifies a Frenchman, as a lion is the emblem of the English nation. Such a device in so noble a pile of building looks like a pun in an heroic poem, and I am very sorry the truly ingenious architect[8] would suffer the statuary[9] to blemish his excellent plan with so poor a conceit. But I hope what I have said will gain quarter for the cock and deliver him out of the lion's paw.

I find likewise in ancient times the conceit of making an echo talk sensibly and give rational answers. If this could be excusable in any writer it would be in Ovid,[10] where he introduces the echo as a nymph before she was worn away into nothing but a voice. The learned Erasmus,[11] though a man of wit and genius, has composed a dialogue upon this silly kind of device and made use of an echo who seems to have been a very extraordinary linguist, for she answers the person she talks with in Latin, Greek, and Hebrew, according as she found the syllables which she was to repeat in any of those learned languages. *Hudibras*, in ridicule of this false kind of wit, has described Bruin bewailing the loss of his bear to a solitary echo, who is of great use to the poet in several distiches, as she does not only repeat after him but helps out his verse and furnishes him with rhymes.

---

5 **Camden** William Camden (1551-1623), historian and antiquary   6 **rebus** word or phrase represented by pictures   7 **Blenheim House** palace of the Duke of Marlborough at Woodstock, Oxfordshire   8 **the truly ingenious architect** Sir John Vanbrugh (1664-1726)   9 **the statuary** Grinling Gibbons (1648-1720)   10 **Ovid** *Metamorphoses* 3.356-69   11 **Erasmus** *Colloquia Familiaria*, "Echo"

He raged and kept as heavy a coil as
Stout Hercules for loss of Hylas,
Forcing the valleys to repeat
The accents of his sad regret.
He beat his breast, and tore his hair,
For loss of his dear crony bear,
That Echo from the hollow ground
His doleful wailings did resound
More wistfully by many times,
Than in small poets' splay-foot rhymes,
That make her, in their rueful stories,
To answer to inter'gatories,
And most unconscionably depose
To things of which she nothing knows:
And when she has said all she can say,
'Tis wrested to the lover's fancy.
Quoth he, O wither, wicked Bruin,
Art thou fled to my—Echo, ruin?
I thought th'hadst scorned to budge a step
For fear. (Quoth Echo) Marry guep.
Am I not here to take thy part!
Then what has quailed thy stubborn heart?
Have these bones rattled, and this head
So often in thy quarrel bled?
Nor did I ever winch or grudge it,
For thy dear sake? (Quoth she) Mum budget.
Think'st thou 'twill not be laid i' th'dish,
Thou turn'dst thy back? Quoth Echo, Pish.
To run from those th' hadst overcome
Thus cowardly? Quoth Echo, Mum.
But what a-vengeance makes thee fly
From me too, as thine enemy?
Or if thou hadst no thought of me
Nor what I have endured for thee,
Yet shame and honor might prevail
To keep thee thus from turning tail:
For who would grudge to spend his blood in
His honor's cause? Quoth she, A puddin.[12]

C

---

12 **He raged . . . puddin** *Hudibras*, Part One (1663), iii, 183-220, by
Samuel Butler

No. 60

[Varieties of false wit]

Wednesday, May 9, 1711

hoc est quod palles? cur quis non prandeat hoc est?—Per.
Sat. 3[1]

The several kinds of false wit that vanished and disappeared in the refined ages of the world discovered themselves again in the times of monkish ignorance.

As the monks were the masters of all that little learning which was then extant and had their whole lives entirely disengaged from business, it is no wonder that several of them who wanted genius for higher performances employed many hours in the composition of such tricks in writing as required much time and little capacity. I have seen half the *Aeneid* turned into Latin rhymes by one of the *beaux esprits* of that dark age, who says in his preface to it that the *Aeneid* wanted nothing but the sweets of rhyme to make it the most perfect work in its kind. I have likewise seen an hymn in hexameters to the Virgin Mary which filled a whole book, though it consisted but of the eight following words:

Tot, tibi, sunt, Virgo, dotes, quot, sidera, caelo.

Thou hast as many virtues, O Virgin, as there are stars
   in Heaven.

1 hoc est . . . hoc est Persius *Satires* 3.85: "Is it over stuff like this that you grow pale? Is it worth while for this to go without your dinner?"

The poet rung the chimes upon these eight several words and by that means made his verses almost as numerous as the virtues and the stars which they celebrated. It is no wonder that men who had so much time upon their hands did not only restore all the antiquated pieces of false wit but enriched the world with inventions of their own. It was to this age that we owe the production of anagrams, which is nothing else but a transmutation of one word into another or the turning of the same set of letters into different words, which may change night into day or black into white if Chance, who is the goddess that presides over these sorts of composition, shall so direct. I remember a witty author in allusion to this kind of writing calls his rival, who (it seems) was distorted and had his limbs set in places that did not properly belong to them, "the anagram of a man."

When the anagrammatist takes a name to work upon, he considers it at first as a mine not broken up, which will not show the treasure it contains till he shall have spent many hours in the search of it; for it is his business to find out one word that conceals itself in another and to examine the letters in all the variety of stations in which they can possibly be ranged. I have heard of a gentleman who, when this kind of wit was in fashion, endeavored to gain his mistress's heart by it. She was one of the finest women of her age and known by the name of the Lady Mary Boon. The lover not being able to make anything of Mary, by certain liberties indulged to this kind of writing converted it into Moll and, after having shut himself up for half a year, with indefatigable industry produced an anagram. Upon the presenting it to his mistress, who was a little vexed in her heart to see herself degraded into Moll Boon, she told him, to his infinite surprise, that he had mistaken her surname, for that it was not Boon but Bohun.

> . . . ibi omnis
> effusus labor . . .[2]

The lover was thunderstruck with his misfortune, in-

---

2 ibi . . . labor Vergil *Georgics* 4.491-2: "In that moment all his toil was spent . . ."

somuch that in a little time after he lost his senses, which indeed had been very much impaired by that continual application he had given to his anagram.

The acrostic was probably invented about the same time with the anagram, though it is impossible to decide whether the inventor of the one or the other was the greater blockhead. The simple acrostic is nothing but the name or title of a person or thing made out of the initial letters of several verses and by that means written, after the manner of the Chinese, in a perpendicular line. But besides these there are compound acrostics, where the principal letters stand two or three deep. I have seen some of them where the verses have not only been edged by a name at each extremity but have had the name running down like a seam through the middle of the poem.

There is another near relation of the anagrams and acrostics which is commonly known by the name of a chronogram. This kind of wit appears very often on many modern medals, especially those of Germany, when they represent in the inscription the year in which they were coined. Thus we see on a medal of Gustaphus Adolphus the following words: ChrIstVs DuX ergo TrIVMphVs. If you take the pains to pick the figures out of the several words and range them in their proper order, you will find they amount to MDCX-VVVII, or 1627, the year in which the medal was stamped; for as some of the letters distinguish themselves from the rest and overtop their fellows, they are to be considered in a double capacity, both as letters and as figures. Your laborious German wits will turn over a whole dictionary for one of these ingenious devices. A man would think they were searching after an apt classical term, but instead of that they are looking out a word that has an L, an M, or a D in it. When therefore we meet with any of these inscriptions, we are not so much to look in 'em for the thought as for the Year of the Lord.

The *bouts rimez* were the favorites of the French nation for a whole age together, and that at a time when it abounded in wit and learning. They were a list of words that rhyme to one another, drawn up by another hand, and given to a poet, who was to make a poem to the rhymes in the same order that they were placed upon the list. The more uncommon the rhymes were, the more extraordinary was the genius of the poet that could accommodate his verses to them. I don't know any greater instance of the decay of wit and learning among the French (which generally follows the declension of empire) than the endeavoring to restore this foolish kind of wit. If the reader will be at the trouble to see examples of it, let him look into the new *Mercure Galant*,[3] where the author every month gives a list of rhymes to be filled up by the ingenious in order to be communicated to the public in the *Mercure* for the succeeding month. That for the month of November, which now lies before me, is as follows.

- Lauriers
- Guerriers
- Musette
- Lisette

- Césars
- Etendars
- Houlette
- Folette

One would be amazed to see so learned a man as Ménage[4] talking seriously on this kind of trifle in the following passage:

> Monsieur de la Chambre has told me that he never knew what he was going to write when he took his pen into his hand, but that one sentence always produced another. For my own part, I never knew what I should write next when I was making verses. In the first place I got all my rhymes together and was afterwards perhaps three or four months in filling them up. I one day showed Monsieur Gombaud a composition of this nature, in which among others I had made use of the four following rhymes, Amaryllis, Phillis, Marne, Arne, desiring him to give me his opinion of it. He told me immediately that my verses were good for nothing. And upon my asking his reason he said, "Because the rhymes are too common and, for that reason, easy to be put into verse." "Marry," says I, "if

3 Mercure Galant periodical founded by Donneau de Visé in 1672   **4 Ménage** Gilles Ménage (1613-1692), French scholar, literary critic, and satirist

it be so, I am very well rewarded for all the pains I have been at." But by Monsieur Gombaud's[5] leave, notwithstanding the severity of the criticism, the verses were good.

Vid. *Menagiana*.[6] Thus far the learned Ménage, whom I have translated word for word.

The first occasion of these *bouts rimez* made them in some manner excusable, as they were tasks which the French ladies used to impose on their lovers. But when a grave author like him above mentioned tasked himself, could there be anything more ridiculous? Or would not one be apt to believe that the author played double[7] and did not make his list of rhymes till he had finished his poem?

I shall only add that this piece of false wit has been finely ridiculed by Monsieur Sarazin[8] in a poem entitled *La Défaite des Bouts-Rimez, The Rout of the Bouts-Rimez*.

I must subjoin to this last kind of wit the double rhymes which are used in doggerel poetry and generally applauded by ignorant readers. If the thought of the couplet in such compositions is good, the rhyme adds nothing to it; and if bad, it will not be in the power of the rhyme to recommend it. I am afraid that great numbers of those who admire the incomparable *Hudibras*[9] do it more on account of these doggerel rhymes than of the parts that really deserve admiration. I am sure I have heard the

> . . . pulpit, drum ecclesiastic,
> Was beat with fist, instead of a stick.

and

> There was an ancient sage philosopher,
> That had read Alexander Ross over,

more frequently quoted than the finest pieces of wit in the whole poem.

C

---

5 Monsier Gombaud Jean-Ogier de Gombauld (1570-1666), French poet   **6 Menagiana I**, 174-5 (third ed., 1713) (Smith). A collection of Ménage's anecdotes and miscellanies, published posthumously   **7 played double** cheated   **8 Monsieur Sarazine** Jean François Sarasin (1603?-1654), French poet   **9 Hudibras** by Samuel Butler, I.i. 11-12, I. ii. 1-2

No. 61

[False wit: punning]

Thursday, May 10, 1711

Non equidem hoc studeo, pullatis ut mihi nugis
pagina turgescat dare pondus idonea fumo.—Pers.[1]

There is no kind of false wit which has been so recommended by the practice of all ages as that which consists in a jingle of words and is comprehended under the general name of punning. It is indeed impossible to kill a weed which the soil has a natural disposition to produce. The seeds of punning are in the minds of all men, and though they may be subdued by reason, reflection, and good sense, they will be very apt to shoot up in the greatest genius that is not broken and cultivated by the rules of art. Imitation is natural to us, and when it does not raise the mind to poetry, painting, music, or other more noble arts, it often breaks out in puns and quibbles.

Aristotle, in the eleventh chapter of his book of rhetoric, describes two or three kinds of puns, which he calls paragrams,[2] among the beauties of good writing and produces instances of them out of some of the greatest authors in the Greek tongue. Cicero has sprinkled several of his works with puns, and in his book where he lays down the rules of oratory quotes abundance of sayings as pieces of wit

---

1 Non equidem . . . fumo Persius *Satires* 5.19-20: "Nay, indeed, it is no aim of mine that my page should swell with pretentious trifles, fit only to give solidity to smoke"   **2 paragrams** word-plays, consisting in the alteration of one letter or group of letters of a word (*OED*)

which also upon examination prove arrant puns. But the age
in which the pun chiefly flourished was the reign of King
James the First. That learned monarch was himself a tolera-
ble punster and made very few bishops or privy councillors
that had not some time or other signalized themselves by a
clinch or a conundrum. It was therefore in this age that the
pun appeared with pomp and dignity. It had before been
admitted into merry speeches and ludicrous compositions
but was now delivered with great gravity from the pulpit or
pronounced in the most solemn manner at the council table.
The greatest authors, in their most serious works, made
frequent use of puns. The sermons of Bishop Andrews[3] and
the tragedies of Shakespeare are full of them. The sinner was
punned into repentance by the former, as in the latter nothing is more usual than to see a hero weeping and quibbling
for a dozen lines together.

I must add to these great authorities, which seem to have
given a kind of sanction to this piece of false wit, that all the
writers of rhetoric have treated of punning with very great
respect and divided the several kinds of it into hard names
that are reckoned among the figures of speech and recommended as ornaments in discourse. I remember a country
schoolmaster of my acquaintance told me once that he had
been in company with a gentleman whom he looked upon
to be the greatest paragrammatist among the moderns.
Upon inquiry I found my learned friend had dined that day
with Mr. Swan,[4] the famous punster, and desiring him to
give me some account of Mr. Swan's conversation he told
me that he generally talked in the paronomasia,[5] that he
sometimes gave into the ploce,[6] but that in his humble
opinion he shined most in the antanaclasis.[7]

I must not here omit that a famous university[8] of this land
was formerly very much infested with puns; but whether or
no this might not arise from the fens and marshes in which

---

3 Bishop Andrews Lancelot Andrewes (1555-1626)   **4 Mr. Swan** a
famous punster also mentioned by Dryden, John Dennis, and
Swift. See *Dryden's Essays*, ed. W. P. Ker (Oxford, 1926), II, 285   **5
paronomasia** pun   **6 ploce** repetition of a word in an altered . . . or
more expressive sense (*OED*)   **7 antanaclasis** the same word repeated in a different, if not a contrary, signification (Samuel
Johnson)   **8 a famous university** Cambridge

it was situated and which are now drained I must leave to the determination of more skillful naturalists.

After this short history of punning, one would wonder how it should be so entirely banished out of the learned world as it is at present, especially since it had found a place in the writings of the most ancient polite authors. To account for this we must consider that the first race of authors, who were the great heroes in writing, were destitute of all rules and arts of criticism, and for that reason, though they excel later writers in greatness of genius, they fall short of them in accuracy and correctness. The moderns cannot reach their beauties but can avoid their imperfections. When the world was furnished with these authors of the first eminence, there grew up another set of writers who gained themselves a reputation by the remarks which they made on the works of those who preceded them. It was one of the employments of these secondary authors to distinguish the several kinds of wit by terms of art and to consider them as more or less perfect according as they were founded in truth. It is no wonder, therefore, that even such authors as Isocrates,[9] Plato, and Cicero should have such little blemishes as are not to be met with in authors of a much inferior character who have written since those several blemishes were discovered. I do not find that there was a proper separation made between puns and fine wit by any of the ancient authors except Quintilian[10] and Longinus.[11] But when this distinction was once settled, it was very natural for all men of sense to agree in it. As for the revival of this false wit, it happened about the time of the revival of letters; but as soon as it was once detected, it immediately vanished and disappeared. At the same time there is no question but, as it has sunk in one age and rose in another, it will again recover itself in some distant period of time, as pedantry and ignorance shall prevail upon wit and sense. And, to speak the truth, I do very much apprehend by some of the last winter's productions, which had their sets of admirers, that our posterity will in a few years degenerate

9 **Isocrates** Athenian orator (436-338 B.C.)   10 **Quintilian** Roman teacher of rhetoric (ca. 35 -ca.95 A.D.), author of the *Institutio Oratoria* on the education of an orator   11 **Longinus** supposed author of the Greek work *On the Sublime* (first or second century A.D.)

into a race of punsters. At least, a man may be very excusable for any apprehensions of this kind that has seen acrostics handed about the town with great secrecy and applause, to which I must also add a little epigram called the *Witches Prayer* that fell into verse when it was read either backward or forward, excepting only that it cursed one way and blessed the other. When one sees there are actually such painstakers among our British wits, who can tell what it may end in? If we must lash one another, let it be with the manly strokes of wit and satire; for I am of the old philosopher's opinion that if I must suffer from one or the other, I would rather it should be from the paw of a lion than the hoof of an ass. I do not speak this out of any spirit of party. There is a most crying dullness on both sides. I have seen Tory acrostics and Whig anagrams and do not quarrel with either of them because they are Whigs or Tories, but because they are anagrams and acrostics.

But to return to punning. Having pursued the history of a pun from its original to its downfall, I shall here define it to be a conceit arising from the use of two words that agree in the sound but differ in the sense. The only way, therefore, to try a piece of wit is to translate it into a different language: if it bears the test, you may pronounce it true; but if it vanishes in the experiment you may conclude it to be a pun. In short, one may say of a pun as the country man described his nightingale, that it is *vox et praeterea nihil*, a sound and nothing but a sound. On the contrary, one may represent true wit by the description which Aristaenetus[12] makes of a fine woman: When she is dressed she is beautiful, when she is undressed she is beautiful; or, as Mercerus has translated it, *Induitur, formosa est: Exuitur, ipsa forma est.*

.C

---

12 Aristaenetus (fl. fifth or sixth century A.D.), Greek letter writer credited with having written two extant collections of love stories in the form of letters

No. 62

[True wit, mixed wit, and false wit]

Friday, May 11, 1711

Scribendi recte sapere est et principium et fons.—Hor.[1]

Mr. Locke has an admirable reflection upon the difference of wit and judgment, whereby he endeavors to show the reason why they are not always the talents of the same person. His words are as follow: "And hence perhaps may be given some reason of that common observation that men who have a great deal of wit and prompt memories have not always the clearest judgment or deepest reason; for wit lying most in the assemblage of ideas and putting those together with quickness and variety, wherein can be found any resemblance or congruity, thereby to make up pleasant pictures and agreeable visions in the fancy; judgment, on the contrary, lies quite on the other side, in separating carefully, one from another, ideas wherein can be found the least difference; thereby to avoid being misled by similitude and by affinity to take one thing for another. This is a way of proceeding quite contrary to metaphor and allusion, wherein for the most part lies that entertainment and pleasantry of wit which strikes so lively on the fancy and therefore is so acceptable to all people. . . ."[2]

This is, I think, the best and most philosophical account

---

1 Scribendi . . . fons Horace *Ars Poetica* 309: "Of good writing the source and fount is wisdom"   **2 "And hence . . . acceptable to all people"** *An Essay Concerning Human Understanding* (1690), Chapter XI: "Of Discerning, and Other Operations of the Mind"

that I have ever met with of wit, which generally, though not always, consists in such a resemblance and congruity of ideas as this author mentions. I shall only add to it by way of explanation that every resemblance of ideas is not that which we call wit unless it be such an one that gives delight and surprise to the reader. These two properties seem essential to wit, more particularly the last of them. In order, therefore, that the resemblance in the ideas be wit, it is necessary that the ideas should not lie too near one another in the nature of things; for where the likeness is obvious, it gives no surprise. To compare one man's singing to that of another or to represent the whiteness of any object by that of milk and snow or the variety of its colors by those of the rainbow cannot be called wit unless, besides this obvious resemblance, there be some further congruity discovered in the two ideas that is capable of giving the reader some surprise. Thus when a poet tells us the bosom of his mistress is as white as snow, there is no wit in the comparison; but when he adds, with a sigh, that it is as cold too, it then grows into wit. Every reader s memory may supply him with innumerable instances of the same nature. For this reason, the similitudes in heroic poets, who endeavor rather to fill the mind with great conceptions than to divert it with such as are new and surprising, have seldom anything in them that can be called wit. Mr. Locke's account of wit, with this short explanation, comprehends most of the species of wit, as metaphors, similitudes, allegories, enigmas, mottoes, parables, fables, dreams, visions, dramatic writings, burlesque, and all the methods of allusion, as there are many other pieces of wit (how remote soever they may appear at first sight from the foregoing description) which upon examination will be found to agree with it.

As true wit generally consists in this resemblance and congruity of ideas, false wit chiefly consists in the resemblance and congruity sometimes of single letters, as in anagrams, chronograms, lipograms, and acrostics; sometimes of syllables, as in echoes and doggerel rhymes; sometimes of words, as in puns and quibbles; and sometimes of whole sentences or poems, cast into the figures of eggs, axes, or altars. Nay, some carry the notion of wit so far as to ascribe it even to external mimicry and to look upon a man as an ingenious person that can resemble the tone, posture, or face of another.

As true wit consists in the resemblance of ideas and false wit in the resemblance of words, according to the foregoing instances, there is another kind of wit which consists partly in the resemblance of ideas and partly in the resemblance of words, which for distinction sake I shall call mixed wit. This kind of wit is that which abounds in Cowley[3] more than in any author that ever wrote. Mr. Waller[4] has likewise a great deal of it. Mr. Dryden is very sparing in it. Milton had a genius much above it. Spenser is in the same class with Milton. The Italians, even in their epic poetry, are full of it. Monsieur Boileau,[5] who formed himself upon the ancient poets, has everywhere rejected it with scorn. If we look after mixed wit among the Greek writers, we shall find it nowhere but in the epigrammatists. There are indeed some strokes of it in the little poem ascribed to Musaeus[6] which by that, as well as many other marks, betrays itself to be a modern composition. If we look into the Latin writers, we find none of this mixed wit in Vergil, Lucretius, or Catullus, very little in Horace, but a great deal of it in Ovid, and scarce anything else in Martial.

Out of the innumerable branches of mixed wit I shall choose one instance which may be met with in all the writers of this class. The passion of love in its nature has been thought to resemble fire, for which reason the words *fire* and *flame* are made use of to signify love. The witty poets therefore have taken an advantage from the doubtful meaning of the word *fire* to make an infinite number of witticisms. Cowley, observing the cold regard of his mistress's eyes[7] and, at the same time, their power of producing love in him, considers them as burning glasses made of ice and, finding himself able to live in the greatest extremities of love, concludes the torrid zone to be habitable. When his

---

3 Cowley Abraham Cowley (1618-1667)   **4 Waller** Edmund Waller (1606-1687)   **5 Boileau** Nicolas Boileau-Despréaux (1636-1711)   **6 Musaeus** the name of two Greek poets: the first pre-Homeric and legendary; the second of the fourth of fifth century A.D.   **7 Cowley . . . mistress's eyes** reference to his collection of poems, ''The Mistress''

mistress has read his letter written in juice of lemon by holding it to the fire, he desires her to read it over a second time by love's flames. When she weeps, he wishes it were inward heat that distilled those drops from the limbeck. When she is absent he is beyond eighty; that is, thirty degrees nearer the pole than when she is with him. His ambitious love is a fire that naturally mounts upward; his happy love is the beams of heaven and his unhappy love flames of hell. When it does not let him sleep, it is a flame that sends up no smoke; when it is opposed by counsel and advice, it is a fire that rages the more by the wind's blowing upon it. Upon the dying of a tree in which he had cut his loves, he observes that his written flames had burnt up and withered the tree. When he resolves to give over his passion, he tells us that one burnt like him forever dreads the fire. His heart is an Aetna that, instead of Vulcan's shop, encloses Cupid's forge in it. His endeavoring to drown his love in wine is throwing oil upon the fire. He would insinuate to his mistress that the fire of love, like that of the sun (which produces so many creatures), should not only warm but beget. Love in another place cooks pleasure at its fire. Sometimes his heart is frozen in every breast and sometimes scorched in every eye. Sometimes he is drowned in tears and burnt in love like a ship set on fire in the middle of the sea.

The reader may observe in every one of these instances that the poet mixes the qualities of fire with those of love, and in the same sentence speaking of it both as a passion and as real fire surprises the reader with those seeming resemblances or contradictions that make up all the wit in this kind of writing. Mixed wit, therefore, is a composition of pun and true wit and is more or less perfect as the resemblance lies in the ideas or in the words. Its foundations are laid partly in falsehood and partly in truth; reason puts in her claim for one half of it and extravagance for the other. The only province, therefore, for this kind of wit is epigram or those little occasional poems that in their own nature are nothing else but a tissue of epigrams. I cannot conclude this head of mixed wit without owning that the admirable poet out of whom I have taken the examples of it had as much true wit as any author that ever writ and indeed all other talents of an extraordinary genius.

It may be expected, since I am upon this subject, that I should take notice of Mr. Dryden's definition[8] of wit, which, with all the deference that is due to the judgment of so great a man, is not so properly a definition of wit as of good writing in general. Wit, as he defines it, is "a propriety of words and thoughts adapted to the subject." If this be a true definition of wit, I am apt to think that Euclid is the greatest wit that ever set pen to paper; it is certain there never was a greater propriety of words and thoughts adapted to the subject than what that author has made use of in his elements. I shall only appeal to my reader if this definition agrees with any notion he has of wit. If it be a true one, I am sure Mr. Dryden was not only a better poet but a greater wit than Mr. Cowley, and Vergil a much more facetious man than either Ovid or Martial.

Bouhours,[9] whom I look upon to be the most penetrating of all the French critics, has taken pains to show that it is impossible for any thought to be beautiful which is not just and has not its foundation in the nature of things, that the basis of all wit is truth, and that no thought can be valuable of which good sense is not the groundwork. Boileau has endeavored to inculcate the same notion in several parts of his writings, both in prose and verse. This is that natural way of writing, that beautiful simplicity, which we so much admire in the compositions of the ancients and which nobody deviates from but those who want strength of genius to make a thought shine in its own natural beauties. Poets who want this strength of genius to give that majestic simplicity to nature which we so much admire in the works of the ancients are forced to hunt after foreign ornaments and not to let any piece of wit of what kind soever escape them. I look upon these writers as Goths in poetry who, like those in architecture, not being able to come up to the beautiful simplicity of the old Greeks and Romans, have endeavored to supply its place with all the extravagances of an irregular fancy. Mr. Dryden makes a very handsome observation on

8 Mr. Dryden's definition in *The Author's Apology for Heroic Poetry and Poetic Licence*, prefixed to *The State of Innocence* (1677). Dryden wrote: "That it is a propriety of thoughts and words; or, in other terms, thoughts and words elegantly adapted to the subject"   **9 Bouhours** Dominique Bouhours (1628-1702)

Ovid's writing a letter from Dido to Aeneas, in the following
words: "Ovid (says he, speaking of Vergil's fiction of Dido
and Aeneas) takes it up after him, even in the same age, and
makes an ancient heroine of Vergil's new-created Dido;
dictates a letter for her, just before her death, to the ungrateful fugitive; and, very unluckily for himself, is for measur-
ing a sword with a man so much superior in force to him, on
the same subject. I think I may be judge of this, because I
have translated both. The famous author of the *Art of Love*
has nothing of his own; he borrows all from a greater master
in his own profession and, which is worse, improves nothing which he finds. Nature fails him; and, being forced to
his old shift, he has recourse to witticism. This passes indeed with his soft admirers and gives him the preference to
Vergil in their esteem."[10]

Were not I supported by so great an authority as that of
Mr. Dryden, I should not venture to observe that the taste of
most of our English poets as well as readers is extremely
Gothic. He quotes Monsieur Segrais[11] for a threefold distinction of the readers of poetry, in the first of which he
comprehends the rabble of readers, whom he does not treat
as such with regard to their quality but to their numbers and
the coarseness of their taste. His words are as follow: "Segrais has distinguished the readers of poetry, according to
their capacity of judging, into three classes. (He might have
said the same of writers too, if he had pleased.) In the lowest
form he places those whom he calls *les petits esprits*—such
things as are our upper-gallery audience in a playhouse,
who like nothing but the husk and rind of wit; prefer a
quibble, a conceit, an epigram before solid sense and elegant expression; these are mob readers. If Vergil and Martial
stood for Parliament men, we know already who would
carry it. But, though they make the greatest appearance in
the field and cry the loudest, the best on't is, they are but a
sort of French Huguenots, or Dutch Boors, brought over in
herds but not naturalized, who have not land of two pounds
per annum in Parnassus and therefore are not privileged to

10 "Ovid . . . Vergil in their esteem" from Dryden's dedicatory
epistle to his translation of the *Aeneid* (1697)   **11 Monsieur Segrais**
Jean Regnauld de Segrais (1624–1701), French translator of Vergil

poll. Their authors are of the same level, fit to represent them on a mountebank's stage or to be masters of the ceremonies in a bear garden. Yet these are they who have the most admirers. But it often happens to their mortification that, as their readers improve their stock of sense (as they may by reading better books and by conversation with men of judgment), they soon forsake them."[12]

I would not break the thread of this discourse with observing that as Mr. Locke in the passage above mentioned has discovered the most fruitful source of wit so there is another of a quite contrary nature to it which does likewise branch itself out into several kinds; for not only the resemblance but the opposition of ideas does very often produce wit, as I could show in several little points, turns, and antitheses that I may possibly enlarge upon in some future speculation.

C

No. 63

[The forms of wit: an allegorical analysis]

Saturday, May 12, 1711

> *Humano capiti cervicem pictor equinam*
> *iungere si velit, et varias inducere plumas*
> *undique collatis membris, ut turpiter atrum*
> *desinat in piscem mulier formosa superne,*
> *spectatum admissi risum teneatis, amici?*

12 "Segrais has distinguished . . . soon forsake them" Dryden in the dedicatory epistle to his translation of the *Aeneid*, referring to Segrais's preface to his own translation

credite, Pisones, isti tabulae fore librum
persimilem, cuius, velut aegri somnia, vanae
fingentur species . . .—Hor.[1]

It is very hard for the mind to disengage itself from a subject
in which it has been long employed. The thoughts will be
rising of themselves from time to time, though we give them
no encouragement, as the tossings and fluctuations of the
sea continue several hours after the winds are laid.

It is to this that I impute my last night's dream or vision,
that formed into one continued allegory the several schemes
of wit, whether false, mixed, or true, that have been the
subject of my late papers.

Methought I was transported into a country that was filled
with prodigies and enchantments, governed by the goddess
of Falsehood, and entitled the Region of False Wit. There
was nothing in the fields, the woods, and the rivers that
appeared natural. Several of the trees blossomed in leaf
gold, some of them produced bone lace, and some of them
precious stones. The fountains bubbled in an opera tune
and were filled with stags, wild boars, and mermaids that
lived among the waters, at the same time that dolphins and
several kinds of fish played upon the banks or took their
pastime in the meadows. The birds had many of them
golden beaks and human voices. The flowers perfumed the
air with smells of incense, ambergris, and pulvillios[2] and
were so interwoven with one another that they grew up in
pieces of embroidery. The winds were filled with sighs and
messages of distant lovers. As I was walking to and fro in
this enchanted wilderness, I could not forbear breaking out
into soliloquies upon the several wonders which lay before
me, when to my great surprise I found there were artificial
echoes in every walk that by repetitions of certain words

1 Humano capiti . . . species Horace *Ars Poetica* 1-8: "If a painter
chose to join a human head to the neck of a horse, and to spread
feathers of many a hue over limbs picked up now here now there, so
that what at the top is a lovely woman ends below in a black and
ugly fish, could you, my friends, if favored with a private view,
refrain from laughing? Believe me, dear Pisos, quite like such
pictures would be a book, whose idle fancies shall be shaped like a
sick man's dreams . . ."   **2 pulvillios** cosmetic or perfumed pow-
der (*OED*)

which I spoke agreed with me or contradicted me in every-thing I said. In the midst of my conversation with these invisible companions, I discovered in the center of a very dark grove a monstrous fabric built after the Gothic manner and covered with innumerable devices in that barbarous kind of sculpture. I immediately went up to it and found it to be a kind of heathen temple consecrated to the god of Dull-ness. Upon my entrance I saw the deity of the place dressed in the habit of a monk with a book in one hand and a rattle in the other. Upon his right hand was Industry, with a lamp burning before her, and on his left Caprice, with a monkey sitting on her shoulder. Before his feet there stood an altar of a very odd make which, as I afterwards found, was shaped in that manner to comply with the inscription that sur-rounded it. Upon the altar there lay several offerings of axes, wings, and eggs, cut in paper and inscribed with verses. The temple was filled with votaries, who applied them-selves to different diversions as their fancies directed them. In one part of it I saw a regiment of Anagrams who were continually in motion, turning to the right or to the left, facing about, doubling their ranks, shifting their stations, and throwing themselves into all the figures and counter-marches of the most changeable and perplexed exercise.

Not far from these was a body of Acrostics made up of very disproportioned persons. It was disposed into three columns, the officers planting themselves in a line on the left hand of each column. The officers were all of them at least six foot high and made three rows of very proper men, but the common soldiers, which filled up the spaces be-tween the officers, were such dwarfs, cripples, and scare-crows that one could hardly look upon them without laugh-ing. There were behind the Acrostics two or three files of Chronograms,[3] which differed only from the former as their officers were equipped (like the figure of Time) with an hourglass in one hand and a scythe in the other and took their posts promiscuously among the private men whom they commanded.

---

3 Chronograms phrases, sentences, or inscriptions, in which cer-tain letters (usually distinguished by size or otherwise from the rest) express by their numerical values a date or epoch (*OED*)

In the body of the temple and before the very face of the
deity methought I saw the phantom of Tryphiodorus[4] the
lipogrammatist[5] engaged in a ball with four and twenty
persons who pursued him by turns through all the intricacies and labyrinths of a country dance without being
able to overtake him.

Observing several to be very busy at the western end of
the temple, I inquired into what they were doing and found
there was in that quarter the great magazine of Rebuses.[6]
These were several things of the most different natures tied
up in bundles and thrown upon one another in heaps like
faggots. You might see an anchor, a night rail,[7] and an
hobbyhorse bound up together. One of the workmen, seeing me very much surprised, told me there was an infinite
deal of wit in several of those bundles and that he would
explain them to me if I pleased. I thanked him for his civility
but told him I was in very great haste at that time. As I was
going out of the temple I observed in one corner of it a
cluster of men and women laughing very heartily and di-
verting themselves at a game of crambo.[8] I heard several
double rhymes as I passed by them, which raised a great
deal of mirth.

Not far from these was another set of merry people engaged at a diversion in which the whole jest was to mistake
one person for another. To give occasion for these ludicrous
mistakes, they were divided into pairs, every pair being
covered from head to foot with the same kind of dress,
though perhaps there was not the least resemblance in their
faces. By this means an old man was sometimes mistaken
for a boy, a woman for a man, and a blackamoor for a
European, which very often produced great peals of laughter. These I guessed to be a party of Puns. But being very
desirous to get out of this world of magic, that had almost
turned my brain, I left the temple and crossed over the fields
that lay about it with all the speed I could make. I was not
gone far before I heard the sound of trumpets and alarms,

4 Tryphiodorus epic poet of the fifth century A.D.   **5 lipogrammatist** writer of compositions which exclude all words
that contain a certain letter or letters (*OED*)   **6 Rebuses** words or
phrases represented by pictures   **7 night rail** dressing gown
(*OED*)   **8 crambo** a game in which one player gives a word or line of
verse to which each of the others has to find a rhyme (*OED*)

that seemed to proclaim the march of an enemy and, as I afterward found, was in reality what I apprehended it. There appeared at a great distance a very shining light and in the midst of it a person of a most beautiful aspect: her name was Truth. On her right hand there marched a male deity, that bore several quivers on his shoulders and grasped several arrows in his hand. His name was Wit. The approach of these two enemies filled all the territories of False Wit with an unspeakable consternation, insomuch that the goddess of those regions appeared in person upon her frontiers with the several inferior deities and the different bodies of forces which I had before seen in the temple, who were now drawn up in array and prepared to give their foes a warm reception. As the march of the enemy was very slow, it gave time to the several inhabitants who bordered upon the Regions of Falsehood to draw their forces into a body with a design to stand upon their guard as neuters and attend the issue of the combat.

I must here inform my reader that the frontiers of the enchanted region which I have before described were inhabited by the species of Mixed Wit, who made a very odd appearance when they were mustered together in an army. There were men whose bodies were stuck full of darts and women whose eyes were burning glasses, men that had hearts of fire and women that had breasts of snow. It would be endless to describe several monsters of the like nature that composed this great army, which immediately fell asunder and divided itself into two parts, the one half throwing themselves behind the banners of Truth and the others behind those of Falsehood.

The goddess of Falsehood was of a gigantic stature and advanced some paces before the front of her army; but as the dazzling light which flowed from Truth began to shine upon her she faded insensibly, insomuch that in a little space she looked rather like an huge phantom than a real substance. At length, as the goddess of Truth approached still nearer to her, she fell away entirely and vanished amidst the brightness of her presence, so that there did not remain the least trace or impression of her figure in the place where she had been seen.

As at the rising of the sun the constellations grow thin and the stars go out one after another till the whole hemisphere is extinguished, such was the vanishing of the goddess; and not only of the goddess herself but of the whole army that attended her, which sympathized with their leader and shrunk into nothing in proportion as the goddess disappeared. At the same time the whole temple sunk, the fish betook themselves to the streams and the wild beasts to the woods, the fountains recovered their murmurs, the birds their voices, the trees their leaves, the flowers their scents, and the whole face of nature its true and genuine appearance. Though I still continued asleep, I fancied myself, as it were, awakened out of a dream when I saw this region of prodigies restored to woods and rivers, fields and meadows.

Upon the removal of that wild scene of wonders, which had very much disturbed my imagination, I took a full survey of the persons of Wit and Truth, for indeed it was impossible to look upon the first without seeing the other at the same time. There was behind them a strong and compact body of figures. The genius of Heroic Poetry appeared with a sword in her hand and a laurel on her head. Tragedy was crowned with a cypress and covered with robes dipped in blood. Satire had smiles in her look and a dagger under her garment. Rhetoric was known by her thunderbolt and Comedy by her mask. After several other figures, Epigram marched up in the rear who had been posted there at the beginning of the expedition that he might not revolt to the enemy, whom he was suspected to favor in his heart. I was very much awed and delighted with the appearance of the god of Wit; there was something so amiable and yet so piercing in his looks as inspired me at once with love and terror. As I was gazing on him to my unspeakable joy, he took a quiver of arrows from his shoulder in order to make me a present of it; but as I was reaching out my hand to receive it of him, I knocked it against a chair and by that means awaked.

C

BALLADS

No. 70

[*Chevy Chase* and epic tradition]

Monday, May 21, 1711

Interdum volgus rectum videt. . .—Hor.[1]

When I traveled I took a particular delight in hearing the songs and fables that are come from father to son and are most in vogue among the common people of the countries through which I passed; for it is impossible that anything should be universally tasted and approved by a multitude, though they are only the rabble of a nation, which hath not in it some peculiar aptness to please and gratify the mind of man. Human nature is the same in all reasonable creatures, and whatever falls in with it will meet with admirers amongst readers of all qualities and conditions. Molière, as we are told by Monsieur Boileau,[2] used to read all his comedies to a little old woman that was his housekeeper as she sat with him at her work by the chimney corner, and could foretell the success of his play in the theater from the reception it met at his fireside; for he tells us the audience always followed the old woman and never failed to laugh in the same place.

1 Interdum . . . videt Horace *Epistles* 2.1.63: "At times the public see straight . . ." **2 Monsieur Boileau** in *Réflexions Critiques . . . sur Longin,* i

I know nothing that more shows the essential and inherent perfection of simplicity of thought above that which I call the Gothic manner in writing than this, that the first pleases all kinds of palates and the latter only such as have formed to themselves a wrong artificial taste upon little fanciful authors and writers of epigram. Homer, Vergil, or Milton, so far as the language of their poems is understood, will please a reader of plain common sense that would neither relish nor comprehend an epigram of Martial or a poem of Cowley. So, on the contrary, an ordinary song or ballad that is the delight of the common people cannot fail to please all such readers as are not unqualified for the entertainment by their affectation or ignorance, and the reason is plain: because the same paintings of nature which recommend it to the most ordinary reader will appear beautiful to the most refined.

The old song of Chevy Chase is the favorite ballad of the common people of England, and Ben Jonson used to say he had rather have been the author of it than of all his works. Sir Philip Sidney, in his discourse of poetry,[3] speaks of it in the following words: "I never heard the old song of Percy and Douglas[4] that I found not my heart moved more than with a trumpet, and yet it is sung by some blind crowder with no rougher voice than rude style; which being so evil appareled in the dust and cobwebs of that uncivil age, what would it work trimmed in the gorgeous eloquence of Pindar?" For my own part, I am so professed an admirer of that antiquated song that I shall give my reader a critique upon it without any further apology for so doing.

The greatest modern critics have laid it down as a rule that a heroic poem should be founded upon some important precept of morality adapted to the constitution of the country in which the poet writes. Homer and Vergil have formed their plans in this view. As Greece was a collection of many governments who suffered very much among themselves and gave the Persian emperor, who was their common enemy, many advantages over them by their mutual jealousies and animosities, Homer, in order to establish among them a union which was so necessary for their

3 **Sir Philip Sidney** in *An Apology for Poetry*   4 **old song of Percy and Douglas** the ballad of *Chevy Chase*

safety, grounds his poem upon the discords of the several Grecian princes who were engaged in a confederacy against an Asiatic prince and the several advantages which the enemy gained by such their discords. At the time the poem we are now treating of was written, the dissentions of the barons, who were then so many petty princes, ran very high, whether they quarreled among themselves or with their neighbors, and produced unspeakable calamities to the country. The poet, to deter men from such unnatural contentions, describes a bloody battle and dreadful scene of death occasioned by the mutual feuds that reigned in the families of an English and Scotch nobleman. That he designed this for the instruction of his poem we may learn from his last four lines, in which, after the example of the modern tragedians, he draws from it a precept for the benefit of his readers.

> God save the King, and bless the land
> In plenty, joy, and peace;
> And grant henceforth that foul debate
> 'Twixt noblemen may cease.

The next point observed by the greatest heroic poets hath been to celebrate persons and actions which do honor to their country. Thus Vergil's hero was the founder of Rome, Homer's a prince of Greece, and for this reason Valerius Flaccus[5] and Statius,[6] who were both Romans, might be justly derided for having chosen the expedition of the Golden Fleece and the wars of Thebes for the subject of their epic writings.

The poet before us has not only found out a hero in his own country but raises the reputation of it by several beautiful incidents. The English are the first that take the field and the last that quit it. The English bring only fifteen hundred to the battle, the Scotch two thousand. The English keep the field with fifty-three; the Scotch retire with fifty-five, all the rest on each side being slain in battle. But the most remarkable circumstance of this kind is the different manner in which the Scotch and English kings receive the news of

---

5 Valerius Flaccus (d. ca. 90 A.D.)   **6 Statius** (ca. 40-ca. 96 A.D.)

this fight and of the great men's deaths who commanded in
it.

> This news was brought to Edinburgh,
>   Where Scotland's king did reign,
> That brave Earl Douglas suddenly
>   Was with an arrow slain.
>
> Oh heavy news, King James did say,
>   Scotland can witness be,
> I have not any captain more
>   Of such account as he.
>
> Like tidings to King Henry came
>   Within as short a space,
> That Percy of Northumberland
>   Was slain in Chevy Chase.
>
> Now God be with him, said our King,
>   Sith 'twill no better be,
> I trust I have within my realm
>   Five hundred as good as he.
>
> Yet shall not Scot nor Scotland say
>   But I will vengeance take,
> And be revenged on them all
>   For brave Lord Percy's sake.
>
> This vow full well the King performed
>   After on Humble-down,
> In one day fifty knights were slain
>   With lords of great renown.
>
> And of the rest of small account
>   Did many thousands die, etc.

At the same time that our poet shows a laudable partiality to
his countrymen, he represents the Scots after a manner not
unbecoming so bold and brave a people.

> Earl Douglas on a milk-white steed,
>   Most like a baron bold,

> Rode foremost of the company
>   Whose armor shone like gold.

His sentiments and actions are every way suitable to a hero. "One of us two," says he, "must die. I am an earl as well as yourself, so that you can have no pretence for refusing the combat. However," says he, " 'tis pity, and indeed would be a sin, that so many innocent men should perish for our sakes; rather let you and I end our quarrel by a single combat."

> E'er thus I will outbraved be,
>   One of us two shall die:
> I know thee well, an earl thou art,
>   Lord Percy, so am I.

> But trust me, Percy, pity it were,
>   And great offence, to kill
> Any of these our harmless men,
>   For they have done no ill.

> Let thou and I the battle try,
>   And set our men aside;
> Accurst be he, Lord Percy said,
>   By whom this is denied.

When these brave men had distinguished themselves in the battle and in single combat with each other, in the midst of a generous parley full of heroic sentiments, the Scotch earl falls and with his dying words encourages his men to revenge his death, representing to them as the most bitter circumstance of it that his rival saw him fall.

> With that there came an arrow keen
>   Out of an English bow,
> Which struck Earl Douglas to the heart
>   A deep and deadly blow.

> Who never spoke more words than these,
>   Fight on my merry men all,
> For why, my life is at an end,
>   Lord Percy sees my fall.

"Merry men," in the language of those times, is no more than a cheerful word for companions and fellow soldiers. A passage in the eleventh book of Vergil's *Aeneid* is very much to be admired, where Camilla[7] in her last agonies, instead of weeping over the wound she had received, as one might have expected from a warrior of her sex, considers only (like the hero of whom we are now speaking) how the battle should be continued after her death.

tum sic exspirans, etc.[8]

(A gathering mist o'erclouds her cheerful eyes,
And from her cheeks the rosy color flies;)
Then turns to her, whom, of her female train,
She trusted most, and thus she speaks with pain:
"Acca, 'tis past! He swims before my sight,
Inexorable Death; and claims his right.
Bear my last words to Turnus: fly with speed,
And bid him timely to my charge succeed,
Repel the Trojans, and the town relieve:
Farewell!" . . .[9]

Turnus did not die in so heroic a manner, though our poet seems to have had his eye upon Turnus's speech in the last verse.

Lord Percy sees my fall.

. . . vicisti, et victum tendere palmas
Ausonii videre . . .[10]

Earl Percy's lamentation over his enemy is generous, beautiful, and passionate. I must only caution the reader not to let the simplicity of the style, which one may well pardon in so old a poet, prejudice him against the greatness of the thought.

---

7 **Camilla** a female warrior who fought against Aeneas   8 **tum . . . exspirans** *Aeneid* 11.820   9 **A gathering mist . . . Farewell** Dryden's translation of the *Aeneid* 11. 1193-1202   10 **vicisti . . . videre** *Aeneid* 12.936-7: "Victor thou art; and as vanquished, have the Ausonians seen me stretch forth my hands"

> Then leaving life Earl Percy took
>> The dead man by the hand,
> And said, Earl Douglas for thy life
>> Would I had lost my land.

> Oh Christ! My very heart doth bleed
>> With sorrow for thy sake;
> For sure a more renowned knight
>> Mischance did never take.

That beautiful line, "Taking the dead man by the hand," will put the reader in mind of Aeneas's behavior towards Lausus, whom he himself had slain as he came to the rescue of his aged father.

> at vero ut voltum vidit morientis et ora,
> ora modis Anchisiades pallentia miris,
> ingemuit miserans graviter dextramque tetendit, etc.[11]

> The pious prince beheld young Lausus dead,
> He grieved; he wept; then grasped his hand, and said,
> Poor hapless youth! What praises can be paid
> To worth so great! . . .[12]

I shall take another opportunity[13] to consider the other parts of this old song.

C

---

11 at vero . . . tetendit *Aeneid* 10.821-3: "But when Anchises' son saw the look on that dying face—that face so pale in wondrous wise—heavily he groaned in pity, and stretched forth his hand . . ." **12 The pious prince . . . great** Dryden's translation (10.1165-70) is as follows:

> The pious prince beheld young Lausus dead,
> He grieved; he wept (the sight an image brought
> Of his own filial love, a sadly pleasing thought),
> Then stretched his hand to hold him up, and said:
> "Poor hapless youth! What praises can be paid
> To love so great" . . .

13 another opportunity in *Spectator* no. 74

No. 74

[*Chevy Chase* and the *Aeneid*]

Friday, May 25, 1711

> . . . *pendent opera interrupta* . . .—Verg.[1]

In my last Monday's paper I gave some general instances of those beautiful strokes that please the reader in the old song of Chevy Chase. I shall here, according to my promise, be more particular and show that the sentiments in that ballad are extremely natural and poetical and full of that majestic simplicity which we admire in the greatest of the ancient poets; for which reason I shall quote several passages of it in which the thought is altogether the same with what we meet in several passages of the *Aeneid*. Not that I would infer from thence that the poet (whoever he was) proposed to himself any imitation of those passages, but that he was directed to them in general by the same kind of poetical genius and by the same copyings after nature.

Had this old song been filled with epigrammatical turns and points of wit, it might perhaps have pleased the wrong taste of some readers, but it would never have become the delight of the common people, nor have warmed the heart of Sir Philip Sidney like the sound of a trumpet. It is only nature that can have this effect and please those tastes which are the most unprejudiced or the most refined. I must, however, beg leave to dissent from so great an authority as that of Sir Philip Sidney in the judgment which he has passed as to the rude style and evil apparel of this anti-

---

1 **pendent . . . interrupta** *Aeneid* 4. 88: ". . . the works are broken off and idle . . ."

quated song, for there are several parts in it where not only the thought but the language is majestic and the numbers very sonorous; at least the apparel is much more gorgeous than many of the poets made use of in Queen Elizabeth's time, as the reader will see in several of the following quotations.

What can be greater than either the thought or the expression in that stanza,

> To drive the deer with hound and horn
>   Earl Percy took his way:
> The child may rue that was unborn
>   The hunting of that day!

This way of considering the misfortunes which this battle would bring upon posterity, not only on those who were born immediately after the battle and lost their fathers in it, but on those also who perished in future battles which should arise from this quarrel of the two earls, is wonderfully beautiful and conformable to the way of thinking among the ancient poets.

> audiet pugnas vitio parentum
> rara iuventus.—Hor.[2]

What can be more sounding and poetical or resemble more the majestic simplicity of the ancients than the following stanzas?

> The stout Earl of Northumberland,
>   A vow to God did make,
> His pleasure in the Scottish woods
>   Three summer's days to take.

> With fifteen hundred bowmen bold,
>   All chosen men of might,
> Who knew full well in time of need,
>   To aim their shafts aright.

---

2 audiet . . . iuventus Horace *Odes* 1.2.23-4: "Our young men, made fewer by the vice of their parents, shall hear of these battles"

The hounds ran swiftly through the woods
　　The nimble deer to take,
And with their cries the hills and dales
　　An echo shrill did make.

. . . vocat ingenti clamore Cithaeron
Taygetique canes domitrixque Epidaurus equorum,
et vox adsensu nemorum ingeminata remugit.[3]

Lo, yonder doth Earl Douglas come,
　　His men in armor bright:
Full twenty hundred Scottish spears,
　　All marching in our sight.

All men of pleasant Tividale,
　　Fast by the river Tweed, etc.

The country of the Scotch warriors described in these two
last verses has a fine romantic situation and affords a couple
of smooth words for verse. If the reader compares the
foregoing six lines of the song with the following Latin
verses, he will see how much they are written in the spirit of
Vergil.

adversi campo apparent hastasque reductis
protendunt longe dextris et spicula vibrant[4]

quique altum Praeneste viri quique arva Gabinae
Iunonis gelidumque Anienem et roscida rivis
Hernica saxa colunt . . .[5]

　　　　　　　　　. . . qui Rosea rura Velini,
qui Tetricae horrentis rupes montemque Severum

---

3 vocat . . . remugit Vergil *Georgics* 3. 43-5: "With mighty clamor
Cithaeron calls, and Taygetus' hounds and Epidaurus, tamer of
horses; and the cry, doubled by the applauding groves, rings
back" **4 adversi . . . vibrant** *Aeneid* 11.605-6: ". . . come into
view, confronting them on the plain; with hands back-drawn
afar, they thrust the lance and brandish the javelin"
5 quique . . . colunt *Aeneid* 7.682-4: ". . . they who dwell in steep
Praeneste, and the fields of Gabine Juno, by the cold Anio and the
Hernican rocks with their dewy streams . . ."

Casperiamque colunt Forulosque et flumen Himellae,
qui Tiberim Fabarimque bibunt . . .[6]

But to proceed.

> Earl Douglas on a milk-white steed,
>   Most like a baron bold,
> Rode foremost of the company
>   Whose armor shone like gold.

Turnus, ut ante volans tardum praecesserat agmen, etc.[7]

vidisti quo Turnus equo, quibus ibat in armis
aureus . . .[8]

> Our English archers bent their bows,
>   Their hearts were good and true;
> At the first flight of arrows sent,
>   Full threescore Scots they slew.

> They closed full fast on ev'ry side,
>   No slackness there was found;
> And many a gallant gentleman
>   Lay gasping on the ground.

> With that there came an arrow keen
>   Out of an English bow,
> Which struck Earl Douglas to the heart
>   A deep and deadly blow.

Aeneas was wounded after the same manner by an unknown hand in the midst of a parley.

> has inter voces, media inter talia verba,

6 qui Rosea . . . bibunt *Aeneid* 7.712-15: ". . . and the Rosean country by Velinus, on Tetrica's rugged crags and Mount Severus, in Casperia and Foruli, and by Himella's stream; they who drink of Tiber and Fabaris . . ." **7 Turnus . . . agmen** *Aeneid* 9.47: "Turnus, as he had flown forward in advance of his tardy column . . ." **8 vidisti . . . aureus** *Aeneid* 9. 269-70: "Thou hast seen the horse and the armor wherewith Turnus rode, all in gold"

ecce viro stridens alis adlapsa sagitta est,
incertum quâ pulsa manu . . .[9]

But of all the descriptive parts of this song there are none
more beautiful than the four following stanzas, which have
a great force and spirit in them and are filled with very
natural circumstances. The thought in the third stanza was
never touched by any other poet and is such a one as would
have shined in Homer or in Vergil.

> So thus did both these nobles die,
>   Whose courage none could stain;
> An English archer then perceived
>   The noble earl was slain.
>
> He had a bow bent in his hand,
>   Made of a trusty tree,
> An arrow of a cloth-yard long
>   Unto the head drew he.
>
> Against Sir Hugh Montgomery
>   So right his shaft he set,
> The grey goose wing that was thereon
>   In his heart blood was wet.
>
> This fight did last from break of day
>   Till setting of the sun;
> For when they rung the evening bell
>   The battle scarce was done.

One may observe likewise that in the catalogue of the slain
the author has followed the example of the greatest ancient
poets, not only in giving a long list of the dead but by
diversifying it with little characters of particular persons.

> And with Earl Douglas there was slain
>   Sir Hugh Montgomery,
> Sir Charles Carrel, that from the field
>   One foot would never fly:

9 has inter voces . . . manu *Aeneid* 12.318-20: "Amid these cries,
amid such words, lo! against him a whizzing arrow winged its way,
launched by what hand . . ."

> Sir Charles Murrel of Ratcliff too,
>> His sister's son was he,
> Sir David Lamb, so well esteemed,
>> Yet saved could not be.

The familiar sound in these names destroys the majesty of the description. For this reason I do not mention this part of the poem but to show the natural turn of thought that appears in it, as the two last verses look almost like a translation of Vergil.

> . . . cadit et Ripheus, iustissimus unus
> qui fuit in Teucris et servantissimus aequi
> (dis aliter visum) . . .[10]

In the catalogue of the English that fell, Witherington's behavior is in the same manner particularized very artfully, as the reader is prepared for it by that account which is given of him in the beginning of the battle.

> Then stepped a gallant squire forth,
>> Witherington was his name,
> Who said, I would not have it told
>> To Henry our King for shame,
> That e'er my Captain fought on foot,
>> And I stood looking on.

We meet with the same heroic sentiments in Vergil.

> non pudet, o Rutuli, pro cunctis talibus unam
> obiectare animam? numerone an viribus aequi
> non sumus? . . .[11]

What can be more natural or more moving than the circumstances in which he describes the behavior of those women who had lost their husbands on this fatal day?

10 cadit . . . visum *Aeneid* 2.426-8: "Ripheus, too, falls, foremost in justice among the Trojans, and most zealous for the right —Heaven's will was otherwise . . ." **11 non pudet . . . sumus** *Aeneid* 12.229-31: " 'Are ye not ashamed, Rutulians, for all a host like ours to set at hazard one single life? In numbers, or in might, are we not their match?' "

Next day did many widows come
    Their husbands to bewail,
They washed their wounds in brinish tears,
    But all would not prevail.

Their bodies bathed in purple blood,
    They bore with them away;
They kissed them dead a thousand times,
    When they were clad in clay.

Thus we see how the thoughts of this poem, which naturally arise from the subject, are always simple and sometimes exquisitely noble, that the language is often very sounding, and that the whole is written with a true poetical spirit.

If this song had been written in the Gothic manner, which is the delight of all our little wits, whether writers or readers, it would not have hit the taste of so many ages and have pleased the readers of all ranks and conditions. I shall only beg pardon for such a profusion of Latin quotations, which I should not have made use of but that I feared my own judgment would have looked too singular on such a subject had not I supported it by the practice and authority of Vergil.

C

No. 85

[*Two Children in the Wood*]

Thursday, June 7, 1711

interdum speciosa locis morataque recte
fabula nullius veneris, sine pondere et arte,
valdius oblectat populum meliusque moratur
quam versus inopes rerum nugaeque canorae.—Hor.[1]

1 interdum speciosa . . . canorae Horace *Ars Poetica* 319-22: "At times a play marked by attractive passages and characters fitly

It is the custom of the Mohammedans if they see any printed or written paper upon the ground to take it up and lay it aside carefully as not knowing but it may contain some piece of their Alkoran. I must confess I have so much of the Mussulman in me that I cannot forbear looking into every printed paper which comes in my way, under whatsoever despicable circumstances it may appear; for as no mortal author in the ordinary fate and vicissitude of things knows to what use his works may sometime or other be applied, a man may oftentimes meet with very celebrated names in a paper of tobacco. I have lighted my pipe more than once with the writings of a prelate and know a friend of mine who, for these several years, has converted the essays of a man of quality into a kind of fringe for his candlesticks. I remember in particular, after having read over a poem of an eminent author on a victory, I met with several fragments of it upon the next rejoicing day which had been employed in squibs and crackers[2] and by that means celebrated its subject in a double capacity. I once met with a page of Mr. Baxter[3] under a Christmas pie. Whether or no the pastry cook had made use of it through chance or waggery for the defense of that superstitious viand[4] I know not, but upon the perusal of it I conceived so good an idea of the author's piety that I bought the whole book. I have often very much profited by these accidental readings and have sometimes found very curious pieces that are either out of print or not to be met with in the shops of our London booksellers. For this reason, when my friends take a survey of my library they are very much surprised to see upon the shelf of folios two long bandboxes[5] standing upright among my books, till I let them see that they are both of them lined with deep erudition and abstruse literature. I might likewise mention a paper kite from which I have received great improvement and a hat case which I would not exchange for all the beavers

sketched, though lacking in charm, though without force and art, gives the people more delight and holds them better than verses void of thought, and sonorous trifles'' **2 squibs and crackers** firecrackers **3 Mr. Baxter** Richard Baxter (1615-1691), Presbyterian clergyman and author **4 superstitious viand** referring to the nonconformist aversion to celebrating holy days **5 bandbox** a cardboard box for collars and hats

in Great Britain. This my inquisitive temper, or rather impertinent humor, of prying into all sorts of writing, with my
natural aversion to loquacity, give me a good deal of employment when I enter any house in the country, for I can't
for my heart leave a room before I have thoroughly studied
the walls of it and examined the several printed papers
which are usually pasted upon them. The last piece that I
met with upon this occasion gave me a most exquisite
pleasure. My reader will think I am not serious when I
acquaint him that the piece I am going to speak of was the
old ballad of the *Two Children in the Wood,* which is one of
the darling songs of the common people and has been the
delight of most Englishmen in some part of their age.

   This song is a plain, simple copy of nature, destitute of all
the helps and ornaments of art. The tale of it is a pretty
tragical story and therefore pleases for no other reason but
because it is a copy of nature. There is even a despicable
simplicity in the verse; and yet, because the sentiments are
natural and unaffected, they are able to move the mind of
the most polite reader with inward meltings of humanity
and compassion. The incidents grow out of the subject and
are such as Vergil himself would have touched upon had the
like story been told by that divine poet. For which reason
the whole narration has something in it very moving, notwithstanding the author of it (whoever he was) has delivered it in such an abject phrase and poorness of expression
that the quoting any part of it would look like a design of
turning it into ridicule. But though the language is mean,
the thoughts from one end to the other are wonderfully
natural and therefore cannot fail to please those who are not
judges of language or those who, notwithstanding they are
judges of language, have a genuine and unprejudiced taste
of nature. The condition, speech, and behavior of the dying
parents, with the age, innocence, and distress of the children, are set forth in such tender circumstances that it is
impossible for a good-natured reader not to be affected with
them. As for the circumstance of the robin redbreast, it is
indeed a little poetical ornament; and to show what a genius
the author was master of amidst all his simplicity, it is just
the same kind of fiction which one of the greatest of the
Latin poets has made use of upon a parallel occasion. I mean
that passage in Horace where he describes himself when he

was a child, fallen asleep in a desert wood and covered with leaves by the turtles[6] that took pity on him.

> me fabulosae Volture in avio
> nutricis extra limen Apuliae
>   ludo fatigatumque somno
>   fronde nova puerum palumbes
> texere . . .[7]

I have heard that the late Lord Dorset,[8] who had the greatest wit tempered with the greatest humanity and was one of the finest critics as well as the best poets of his age, had a numerous collection of Old English ballads and took a particular pleasure in the reading of them. I can affirm the same of Mr. Dryden and know several of the most refined writers of our present age who are of the same humor.

I might likewise refer my reader to Molière's thoughts on this subject as he has expressed them in the character of the misanthrope;[9] but those only who are endowed with a true greatness of soul and genius can divest themselves of the little images of ridicule and admire nature in her simplicity and nakedness. As for the little conceited wits of the age who can only show their judgment by finding fault, they cannot be supposed to admire these productions that have nothing to recommend them but the beauties of nature, when they do not know how to relish even those compositions that, with all the beauties of nature, have also the additional advantages of art.   L

---

6 turtles turtledoves   **7 me fabulosae . . . texere** Horace *Odes* 3.4.9-13: "In childhood days, on trackless Vultur, beyond the borders of old nurse Apulia, when I was tired with play and overcome with sleep, the doves of story covered me o'er with freshly fallen leaves . . ."   **8 Lord Dorset** Charles Sackville, sixth Earl of Dorset (1638-1706)   **9 misanthrope** in *Le Misanthrope* (1666)

GENIUS

No. 160*

[The nature of genius]

Monday, September 3, 1711

> . . . cui mens divinior atque os
> magna sonaturum, des nominis huius honorem.—Hor.[1]

There is no character more frequently given to a writer than
that of being a genius. I have heard many a little sonneteer
called a "fine genius." There is not an heroic scribbler in the
nation that has not his admirers who think him a "great
genius," and as for your smatterers in tragedy there is scarce
a man among them who is not cried up by one or other for a
"prodigious genius."

My design in this paper is to consider what is properly a
great genius and to throw some thoughts together on so
uncommon a subject.

Among great geniuses those few draw the admiration of
all the world upon them and stand up as the prodigies of
mankind who by the mere strength of natural parts and
without any assistance of art or learning have produced
works that were the delight of their own times and the

---

*No. 161 in the first edition; changed to 160 in the collected edi-
tions.
1 cui mens . . . honorem Horace *Satires* 1.4.43-4: " . . . if one has a
soul divine and tongue of noble utterance, to such give the honor of
that name"

wonder of posterity. There appears something nobly wild and extravagant in these great natural geniuses that is infinitely more beautiful than all the turn and polishing of what the French call a *bel esprit*, by which they would express a genius refined by conversation, reflection, and the reading of the most polite authors. The greatest genius that runs through the arts and sciences takes a kind of tincture from them and falls unavoidably into imitation.

Many of these great natural geniuses that were never disciplined and broken by rules of art are to be found among the ancients and in particular among those of the more eastern parts of the world. Homer has innumerable flights that Vergil was not able to reach, and in the Old Testament we find several passages more elevated and sublime than any in Homer. At the same time that we allow a greater and more daring genius to the ancients we must own that the greatest of them very much failed in or, if you will, that they were very much above the nicety and correctness of the moderns. In their similitudes and allusions, provided there was a likeness, they did not much trouble themselves about the decency of the comparison; thus Solomon resembles the nose of his beloved to the Tower of Lebanon which looketh toward Damascus,[2] as the coming of a thief in the night[3] is a similitude of the same kind in the New Testament. It would be endless to make collections of this nature; Homer illustrates one of his heroes encompassed with the enemy by an ass in a field of corn that has his sides belabored by all the boys of the village without stirring a foot for it and another of them tossing to and fro in his bed and burning with resentment to a piece of flesh broiling on the coals.[4] This particular failure in the ancients opens a large field of raillery to the little wits, who can laugh at an indecency but not relish the sublime in these sorts of writings. The present Emperor of Persia, conformable to this eastern way of thinking, amidst a great many pompous titles denominates himself the Sun of Glory and the Nutmeg of Delight. In short, to cut off all caviling against the ancients and particularly those of the warmer climates who had most heat and life in their

---

2 Solomon resembles . . . Damascus Song of Solomon 7:4
3 coming of . . . night 2 Peter 3:10   **4 Homer illustrates . . . coals**
Iliad 11.558-65; *Odyssey* 20.25-30

imaginations, we are to consider that the rule of observing what the French call the *bienséance*[5] in an allusion has been found out of latter years and in the colder regions of the world where we would make some amends for our want of force and spirit by a scrupulous nicety and exactness in our compositions. Our countryman Shakespeare was a remarkable instance of this first kind of great geniuses.

I cannot quit this head without observing that Pindar was a great genius of the first class who was hurried on by a natural fire and impetuosity to vast conceptions of things and noble sallies of imagination. At the same time, can anything be more ridiculous than for men of a sober and moderate fancy to imitate this poet's way of writing in those monstrous compositions which go among us under the name of pindarics? When I see people copying works which, as Horace has represented them, are singular in their kind and inimitable, when I see men following irregularities by rule and by the little tricks of art straining after the most unbounded flights of nature, I cannot but apply to them that passage in Terence.

> . . . incerta haec si tu postules
> ratione certa facere, nihilo plus agas
> quam si des operam ut cum ratione insanias.[6]

In short, a modern Pindaric writer compared with Pindar is like a sister among the Camisars[7] compared with Vergil's Sybil. There is the distortion, grimace, and outward figure, but nothing of that divine impulse which raises the mind above itself and makes the sounds more than human.

The second class of great geniuses are those that have formed themselves by rules and submitted the greatness of their natural talents to the corrections and restraints of art. Such among the Greeks were Plato and Aristotle, among the Romans Vergil and Tully, among the English Milton and Sir

---

5 bienséance decorum, propriety **6 incerta . . . insanias** *Eunuchus* 1.61-3: "If you tried to turn these uncertainties into certainties by a system of reasoning, you'd do no more good than if you set yourself to be mad on a system" **7 Camisars** name given to the Calvinist insurgents of the Cévennes, during the persecution which followed the revocation of the edict of Nantes (*OED*)

Francis Bacon. The genius in both these classes of authors may be equally great but shows itself in a different manner. In the first it is like a rich soil in a happy climate that produces a whole wilderness of noble plants rising in a thousand beautiful landscapes without any certain order or regularity. In the other it is the same rich soil under the same happy climate that has been laid out in walks and parterres and cut into shape and beauty by the skill of the gardener.

The great danger in these latter kind of geniuses is lest they cramp their own abilities too much by imitation and form themselves altogether upon models without giving the full play to their own natural parts. An imitation of the best authors is not to compare with a good original, and I believe we may observe that very few writers make an extraordinary figure in the world who have not something in their way of thinking or expressing themselves that is peculiar to them and entirely their own. It is odd to consider what great geniuses are sometimes thrown away upon trifles.

I once saw a shepherd, says a famous Italian author, that used to divert himself in his solitudes with tossing up eggs and catching them again without breaking them, in which he had arrived to so great a degree of perfection that he would keep up four at a time for several minutes together, playing in the air and falling into his hands by turns. I think, says the author, I never saw a greater severity than in this man's face; for by his wonderful perseverance and application he had contracted the seriousness and gravity of a privy councillor, and I could not but reflect with myself that the same assiduity and attention, had they been rightly applied, would have made him a greater mathematician than Archimedes.[8]

C

8 **Archimedes** Greek mathematician (287?-212 B.C.)

MILTON

No. 267

[The "fable" of *Paradise Lost*]

Saturday, January 5, 1712

cedite Romani scriptores, cedite Grai.—Propert.[1]

There is nothing in nature so irksome as general discourses, especially when they turn chiefly upon words. For this reason I shall waive the discussion of that point which was started some years since, whether Milton's *Paradise Lost* may be called an heroic poem. Those who will not give it that title may call it (if they please) a divine poem. It will be sufficient to its perfection if it has in it all the beauties of the highest kind of poetry, and as for those who say it is not an heroic poem, they advance no more to the diminution of it than if they should say Adam is not Aeneas nor Eve Helen.

I shall therefore examine it by the rules of epic poetry and see whether it falls short of the *Iliad* or *Aeneid* in the beauties which are essential to that kind of writing. The first thing to be considered in an epic poem is the fable, which is perfect or imperfect according as the action which it relates is more or less so. This action should have three qualifications in it. First, it should be but one action. Secondly, it should be an entire action; and thirdly, it should be a great action.

To consider the action of the *Iliad*, *Aeneid*, and *Paradise Lost* in these three several lights: Homer, to preserve the unity of his action, hastens into the midst of things as Horace has observed.[2] Had he gone up to Leda's egg or

1 **cedite . . . Grai** Propertius *Elegies* 2.34.65: "Yield ye, bards of Rome, yield ye, singers of Greece!"   2 **as Horace has observed** *Ars Poetica* 147

begun much later, even at the rape of Helen or the investing of Troy, it is manifest that the story of the poem would have been a series of several actions. He therefore opens his poem with the discord of his princes and with great art interweaves in the several succeeding parts of it an account of everything which relates to the story and had passed before that fatal dissention. After the same manner Aeneas makes his first appearance in the Tyrrhene seas and within sight of Italy because the action proposed to be celebrated was that of his settling himself in Latium. But because it was necessary for the reader to know what had happened to him in the taking of Troy and in the preceding parts of his voyage, Vergil makes his hero relate it by way of episode in the second and third books of the *Aeneid*, the contents of both which books come before those of the first book in the thread of the story, though for the preserving of this unity of action they follow them in the disposition of the poem. Milton, in imitation of these two great poets, opens his *Paradise Lost* with an infernal council plotting the fall of man, which is the action he proposed to celebrate, and as for those great actions which preceded in point of time, the battle of the angels and the creation of the world (which would have entirely destroyed the unity of his principal action had he related them in the same order that they happened), he cast them into the fifth, sixth, and seventh books by way of episode to this noble poem.

Aristotle himself allows that Homer[3] has nothing to boast of as to the unity of his fable, though at the same time that great critic and philosopher endeavors to palliate this imperfection in the Greek poet by imputing it in some measure to the very nature of an epic poem. Some have been of opinion that the *Aeneid* labors also in this particular and has episodes which may be looked upon as excrescencies rather than as parts of the action. On the contrary, the poem which we have now under our consideration hath no other episodes than such as naturally arise from the subject and yet is filled with such a multitude of astonishing circumstances that it gives us at the same time a pleasure of the greatest variety and of the greatest simplicity.

I must observe also that as Vergil in the poem which was

3 **Aristotle . . . Homer** *Poetics* 26.12-15

designed to celebrate the original of the Roman Empire has
described the birth of its great rival, the Carthaginian
Commonwealth, Milton with the like art in his poem on the
fall of man has related the fall of those angels who are his
professed enemies. Besides the many other beauties in such
an episode, its running parallel with the great action of the
poem hinders it from breaking the unity so much as another
episode would have done that had not so great an affinity
with the principal subject. In short, this is the same kind of
beauty which the critics admire in *The Spanish Friar* or *The
Double Discovery*, where the two different plots look like
counterparts and copies of one another.

The second qualification required in the action of an epic
poem is that it should be an entire action. An action is entire
when it is complete in all its parts or, as Aristotle describes
it, when it consists of a beginning, a middle, and an end.
Nothing should go before it, be intermixed with it, or follow
after it that is not related to it, as on the contrary no single
step should be omitted in that just and regular progress
which it must be supposed to take from its original to its
consummation. Thus we see the anger of Achilles in its
birth, its continuance and effects, and Aeneas's settlement
in Italy carried on through all the oppositions in his way to it
both by sea and land. The action in Milton excels (I think)
both the former in this particular; we see it contrived in hell,
executed upon earth, and punished by heaven. The parts of
it are told in the most distinct manner and grow out of one
another in the most natural method.

The third qualification of an epic poem is its greatness.
The anger of Achilles was of such consequence that it em-
broiled the kings of Greece, destroyed the heroes of Troy,
and engaged all the gods in factions. Aeneas's settlement in
Italy produced the Caesars and gave birth to the Roman
Empire. Milton's subject was still greater than either of the
former; it does not determine the fate of single persons or
nations but of a whole species. The united powers of hell are
joined together for the destruction of mankind, which they
effected in part and would have completed had not Om-
nipotence itself interposed. The principal actors are Man in
his greatest perfection and Woman in her highest beauty.
Their enemies are the fallen angels, the Messiah their
friend, and the Almighty their protector. In short, every-

thing that is great in the whole circle of being, whether within the verge of nature or out of it, has a proper part assigned it in this noble poem.

In poetry, as in architecture, not only the whole but the principal members and every part of them should be great. I will not presume to say that the Book of Games in the *Aeneid*[4] or that in the *Iliad*[5] are not of this nature, nor to reprehend Vergil's simile of a top[6] and many other of the same nature in the *Iliad* as liable to any censure in this particular, but I think we may say without offence to those wonderful performances that there is an unquestionable magnificence in every part of *Paradise Lost* and indeed a much greater than could have been formed upon any pagan system.

But Aristotle by the greatness of the action does not only mean that it should be great in its nature but also in its duration or, in other words, that it should have a due length in it as well as what we properly call greatness. The just measure of this kind of magnitude he explains by the following similitude:[7] an animal no bigger than a mite cannot appear perfect to the eye because the sight takes it in at once and has only a confused idea of the whole and not a distinct idea of all its parts; if on the contrary you should suppose an animal of ten thousand furlongs in length, the eye would be so filled with a single part of it that it could not give the mind an idea of the whole. What these animals are to the eye a very short or a very long action would be to the memory; the first would be, as it were, lost and swallowed up by it and the other difficult to be contained in it. Homer and Vergil have shown their principal art in this particular; the action of the *Iliad* and that of the *Aeneid* were in themselves exceeding short but are so beautifully extended and diversified by the intervention of episodes and the machinery of gods with the like poetical ornaments that they make up an agreeable story sufficient to employ the memory without overcharging it. Milton's action is enriched with such a variety of circumstances that I have taken as much pleasure in reading the contents of his books as in the best invented story I ever

---

4 **Book of Games in the Aeneid** Book 5   5 **Book of Games in the Iliad** Book 23   6 **Vergil's . . . top** *Aeneid* 7.378-84   7 **Aristotle . . . similitude** *Poetics* 7.4

met with. It is possible that the traditions on which the *Iliad*
and *Aeneid* were built had more circumstances in them than
the history of the fall of man as it is related in Scripture.
Besides it was easier for Homer and Vergil to dash the truth
with fiction, as they were in no danger of offending the
religion of their country by it. But as for Milton, he had not
only a very few circumstances upon which to raise his poem
but was also obliged to proceed with the greatest caution in
everything that he added out of his own invention. And,
indeed, notwithstanding all the restraints he was under, he
has filled his story with so many surprising incidents which
bear so close an analogy with what is delivered in Holy Writ
that it is capable of pleasing the most delicate reader without giving offence to the most scrupulous.

   The modern critics have collected from several hints in the
Iliad and *Aeneid* the space of time which is taken up by the
action of each of those poems; but as a great part of Milton's
story was transacted in regions that lie out of the reach of the
sun and the sphere of day, it is impossible to gratify the
reader with such a calculation, which indeed would be more
curious than instructive, none of the critics either ancient or
modern having laid down rules to circumscribe the action of
an epic poem with any determined number of years, days,
or hours.

   This piece of criticism on Milton's *Paradise Lost* shall be
carried on in following papers.

L

No. 273

[The characters of *Paradise Lost*]

Saturday, January 12, 1712

> . . . *notandi sunt tibi mores*—Hor.[1]

1 notandi . . . mores Horace *Ars Poetica* 156: "note the manners"

Having examined the action of *Paradise Lost*, let us in the next place consider the actors. These are what Aristotle means by the fable and the manners or, as we generally call them in English, the fable and the characters.

Homer has excelled all the heroic poets that ever wrote in the multitude and variety of his characters. Every god that is admitted into his poem acts a part which would have been suitable to no other deity. His princes are as much distinguished by their manners as by their dominions, and even those among them whose characters seem wholly made up of courage differ from one another as to the particular kinds of courage in which they excel. In short, there is scarce a speech or action in the *Iliad* which the reader may not ascribe to the person that speaks or acts without seeing his name at the head of it.

Homer does not only outshine all other poets in the variety but also in the novelty of his characters. He has introduced among his Grecian princes a person who had lived thrice the age of man[2] and conversed with Theseus, Hercules, Polyphemus, and the first race of heroes. His principal actor is the offspring of a goddess, not to mention the son of Aurora who has likewise a place in his poem and the venerable Trojan prince who was the father of so many kings and heroes. There is in these several characters of Homer a certain dignity as well as novelty which adapts them in a more peculiar manner to the nature of an heroic poem, though at the same time, to give them the greater variety, he has described a Vulcan that is the buffoon among his gods and a Thersites among his mortals.

Vergil falls infinitely short of Homer in the characters of his poem, both as to their variety and novelty. Aeneas is indeed a perfect character, but as for Achates, though he is styled the hero's friend, he does nothing in the whole poem which may deserve that title. Gias, Mnesteus, Sergestus, and Cloanthus are all of them men of the same stamp and character,

> fortemque Gyan fortemque Cloanthum[3]

There are indeed several very natural incidents in the part of

---

2 **a person . . . age of man** Nestor   3 **fortemque . . . Cloanthum**
Aeneid 1.222 and 612: ". . . brave Gyas, and brave Cloanthus"

Ascanius, as that of Dido cannot be sufficiently admired. I do not see anything new or particular in Turnus. Pallas and Evander are copies of Hector and Priam, as Lausus and Mezentius are almost parallels to Pallas and Evander. The characters of Nisus and Eurialus are beautiful but common. In short, there is neither that variety nor novelty in the persons of the *Aeneid* which we meet with in those of the *Iliad*.

If we look into the characters of Milton, we shall find that he has introduced all the variety that his poem was capable of receiving. The whole species of mankind was in two persons at the time to which the subject of his poem is confined. We have, however, four distinct characters in these two persons. We see Man and Woman in the highest innocence and perfection and in the most abject state of guilt and infirmity. The two last characters are, indeed, very common and obvious, but the two first are not only more magnificent but more new than any characters either in Vergil or Homer or indeed in the whole circle of nature.

Milton was so sensible of this defect in the subject of his poem and of the few characters it would afford him that he has brought into it two actors of a shadowy and fictitious nature in the persons of Sin and Death, by which means he has interwoven in the body of his fable a very beautiful and well-invented allegory. But notwithstanding the fineness of this allegory may atone for it in some measure, I cannot think that persons of such a chimerical existence are proper actors in an epic poem because there is not that measure of probability annexed to them which is requisite in writings of this kind.

Vergil has, indeed, admitted Fame as an actress in the *Aeneid*, but the part she acts is very short and none of the most admired circumstances in that divine work. We find in mock-heroic poems, particularly in *The Dispensary* and *The Lutrin*,[4] several allegorical persons of this nature, which are very beautiful in those compositions and may, perhaps, be used as an argument that the authors of them were of opinion that such characters might have a place in an epic work. For my own part, I should be glad the reader would think so

4 The Dispensary (1699), by Sir Samuel Garth; **The Lutrin** (1674 and 1683), by Boileau

for the sake of the poem I am now examining and must further add that if such empty, unsubstantial beings may be ever made use of on this occasion there were never any more nicely imagined and employed in more proper actions than those of which I am now speaking.

Another principal actor in this poem is the great enemy of mankind. The part of Ulysses in Homer's *Odyssey* is very much admired by Aristotle[5] as perplexing that fable with very agreeable plots and intricacies, not only by the many adventures in his voyage and the subtlety of his behavior but by the various concealments and discoveries of his person in several parts of that poem. But the crafty being I have now mentioned makes a much longer voyage than Ulysses, puts in practice many more wiles and stratagems, and hides himself under a great variety of shapes and appearances, all of which are severally detected to the great delight and surprise of the reader.

We may likewise observe with how much art the poet has varied several characters of the persons that speak in his infernal assembly. On the contrary, how has he represented the whole Godhead exerting itself towards man in its full benevolence under the threefold distinction of a Creator, a Redeemer, and a Comforter!

Nor must we omit the person of Raphael, who amidst his tenderness and friendship for man shows such a dignity and condescension in all his speech and behavior as are suitable to a superior nature.

There is another circumstance in the principal actors of the *Iliad* and *Aeneid* which gives a particular beauty to those two poems and was therefore contrived with very great judgment. I mean the authors having chosen for their heroes persons who were so nearly related to the people for whom they wrote. Achilles was a Greek and Aeneas the remote founder of Rome. By this means their countrymen (whom they principally proposed to themselves for their readers) were particularly attentive to all the parts of their story and sympathized with their heroes in all their adventures. A Roman could not but rejoice in the escapes, successes, and victories of Aeneas and be grieved at any defeats, misfortunes, or disappointments that befell him, as a Greek

5 Ulysses . . . **Aristotle** *Poetics* 17 and 24

must have had the same regard for Achilles. And it is plain that each of those poems have lost this great advantage among those readers to whom their heroes are as strangers or indifferent persons.

Milton's poem is admirable in this respect, since it is impossible for any of its readers, whatever nation, country, or people he may belong to, not to be related to the persons who are the principal actors in it. But what is still infinitely more to its advantage, the principal actors in this poem are not only our progenitors but our representatives. We have an actual interest in everything they do, and no less than our utmost happiness or misery is concerned and lies at stake in all their behavior.

I shall subjoin as a corollary to the foregoing remark an admirable observation out of Aristotle which hath been very much misrepresented in the quotations of some modern critics. "If a man of perfect and consummate virtue falls into a misfortune, it raises our pity but not our terror because we do not fear that it may be our own case who do not resemble the suffering person."[6] But as that great philosopher adds, "If we see a man of virtues mixed with infirmities fall into any misfortune, it does not only raise our pity but our terror because we are afraid that the like misfortunes may happen to ourselves who resemble the character of the suffering person."

I shall take another opportunity to observe that a person of an absolute and consummate virtue should never be introduced in tragedy and shall only remark in this place that this observation of Aristotle, though it may be true in other occasions, does not hold in this, because in the present case, though the persons who fall into misfortune are of the most perfect and consummate virtue, it is not to be considered as what may possibly be but what actually is our own case, since we are embarked with them on the same bottom and must be partakers of their happiness or misery.

In this and some other few instances Aristotle's rules for epic poetry (which he had drawn from his reflections upon Homer) cannot be supposed to quadrate exactly with the heroic poems which have been made since his time, as it is plain his rules would have been still more perfect could he

6 If a man . . . person *Poetics* 13.2-3

have perused the *Aeneid* which was made some hundred years after his death.

In my next I shall go through other parts of Milton's poem and hope that what I shall there advance, as well as what I have already written, will not only serve as a comment upon Milton but upon Aristotle.

L

No. 279

[The "sentiments" of *Paradise Lost*]

Saturday, January 19, 1712

reddere personae scit convenientia cuique.—Hor.[1]

We have already taken a general survey of the fable and characters in Milton's *Paradise Lost*; the parts which remain to be considered, according to Aristotle's method, are the sentiments and the language. Before I enter upon the first of these, I must advertise my reader that it is my design as soon as I have finished my general reflections on these four several heads to give particular instances out of the poem which is now before us of beauties and imperfections which may be observed under each of them as also of such other particulars as may not properly fall under any of them. This I thought fit to premise that the reader may not judge too hastily of this piece of criticism or look upon it as imperfect before he has seen the whole extent of it.

The sentiments in an epic poem are the thoughts and behavior which the author ascribes to the persons whom he introduces and are just when they are conformable to the

---

1 reddere . . . cuique Horace *Ars Poetica* 316: "He knows how to give each character his fitting part"

characters of the several persons. The sentiments have likewise a relation to things as well as persons and are then perfect when they are such as are adapted to the subject. If in either of these cases the poet argues or explains, magnifies or diminishes, raises love or hatred, pity or terror, or any other passion, we ought to consider whether the sentiments he makes use of are proper for these ends. Homer is censured by the critics for his defect as to this particular in several parts of the *Iliad* and *Odyssey*, though at the same time those who have treated this great poet with candor have attributed this defect to the times in which he lived. It was the fault of the age and not of Homer if there wants that delicacy in some of his sentiments which appears in the works of men of a much inferior genius. Besides, if there are blemishes in any particular thoughts, there is an infinite beauty in the greatest part of them. In short, if there are many poets who would not have fallen into the meanness of some of his sentiments, there are none who could have risen up to the greatness of others. Vergil has excelled all others in the propriety of his sentiments. Milton shines likewise very much in this particular, nor must we omit one consideration which adds to his honor and reputation. Homer and Vergil introduced persons whose characters are commonly known among men and such as are to be met with either in history or in ordinary conversation; Milton's characters, most of them, lie out of nature and were to be formed purely by his own invention. It shows a greater genius in Shakespeare to have drawn his Caliban than his Hotspur or Julius Caesar; the one was to be supplied out of his own imagination, whereas the other might have been formed upon tradition, history, and observation. It was much easier therefore for Homer to find proper sentiments for an assembly of Grecian generals than for Milton to diversify his infernal council with proper characters and inspire them with a variety of sentiments. The loves of Dido and Aeneas are only copies of what has passed between other persons. Adam and Eve before the fall are a different species from that of mankind who are descended from them, and none but a poet of the most unbounded invention and the most exquisite judgment could have filled their conversation and behavior with such beautiful circumstances during their state of innocence.

Nor is it sufficient for an epic poem to be filled with such thoughts as are natural, unless it abound also with such as are sublime. Vergil in this particular falls short of Homer. He has not indeed so many thoughts that are low and vulgar, but at the same time not so many thoughts that are sublime and noble. The truth of it is, Vergil seldom rises into very astonishing sentiments where he is not fired by the *Iliad*. He everywhere charms and pleases us by the force of his own genius but seldom elevates and transports us where he does not fetch his hints from Homer.

Milton's chief talents and indeed his distinguishing excellence lies in the sublimity of his thoughts. There are others of the moderns who rival him in every other part of poetry, but in the greatness of his sentiments he triumphs over all the poets both modern and ancient, Homer only excepted. It is impossible for the imagination of man to distend itself with greater ideas than those which he has laid together in his first and sixth book. The seventh, which describes the creation of the world, is likewise wonderfully sublime, though not so apt to stir up emotion in the mind of the reader nor consequently so perfect in the epic way of writing because it is filled with less action. Let the reader compare what Longinus has observed in several passages in Homer,[2] and he will find parallels for most of them in the *Paradise Lost*.

From what has been said, we may infer that as there are two kinds of sentiments, the natural and the sublime, which are always to be pursued in an heroic poem, there are also two kinds of thoughts which are carefully to be avoided. The first are such as are affected and unnatural; the second such as are mean and vulgar. As for the first kind of thoughts we meet with little or nothing that is like them in Vergil. He has none of those little points and puerilities that are so often to be met with in Ovid, none of the epigrammatic turns of Lucan, none of those swelling sentiments which are so frequent in Statius and Claudian, none of those mixed embellishments of Tasso. Everything is just and natural. His sentiments show that he had a perfect insight into human nature and that he knew everything which was the most proper to affect it. I remember but one line in him

2 **Longinus . . . Homer** *On the Sublime* 9

which has been objected against by the critics as a point of wit. It is in his ninth book where Juno, speaking of the Trojans—how they survived the ruins of their city —expresses herself in the following words:

> num capti potuere capi, num incensa cremarunt pergama? . . .[3]

Were the Trojans taken even after they were captives,
Or did Troy burn even when it was in flames?

Mr. Dryden has in some places, which I may hereafter take notice of, misrepresented Vergil's way of thinking as to this particular in the translation he has given us of the *Aeneid*. I do not remember that Homer anywhere falls into the faults above mentioned, which were indeed the false refinements of later ages. Milton, it must be confessed, has sometimes erred in this respect, as I shall show more at large in another paper, though considering how all the poets of the age in which he writ were infected with this wrong way of thinking, he is rather to be admired that he did not give more into it than that he did sometimes comply with that vicious taste which prevails so much among modern writers.

But since several thoughts may be natural which are low and groveling, an epic poet should not only avoid such sentiments as are unnatural or affected but also such as are low and vulgar. Homer has opened a great field of raillery to men of more delicacy than greatness of genius by the homeliness of some of his sentiments. But, as I have before said, these are rather to be imputed to the simplicity of the age in which he lived, to which I may also add, of that which he described, than to any imperfection in that divine poet. Zoilus[4] among the ancients and Monsieur Perrault[5] among the moderns pushed their ridicule very far upon him on account of some such sentiments. There is no blemish to be observed in Vergil under this head and but very few in Milton.

3 **num . . . pergama** Addison is in error. See *Aeneid* 7.295-6 as follows: "num capti potuere capi? num incensa cremavit Troia viros? . . ."   4 **Zoilus** Greek grammarian of antiquity, whose name came to stand for a faultfinding critic   5 **Monsieur Perrault** Charles Perrault (1628-1703), critic and poet

I shall give but one instance of this impropriety of sentiments in Homer and at the same time compare it with an
instance of the same nature both in Vergil and Milton.
Sentiments which raise laughter can very seldom be admitted with any decency into an heroic poem, whose business
it is to excite passions of a much nobler nature. Homer,
however, in his characters of Vulcan and Thersites, in his
story of Mars and Venus, in his behavior of Irus, and in
other passages, has been observed to have lapsed into the
burlesque character and to have departed from that serious
air which seems essential to the magnificence of an epic
poem. I remember but one laugh in the whole *Aeneid*, which
rises in the fifth book upon Menoetes, where he is represented as thrown overboard and drying himself upon a
rock. But this piece of mirth is so well timed that the severest
critic can have nothing to say against it, for it is in the Book
of Games and Diversions, where the reader's mind may be
supposed to be sufficiently relaxed for such an entertainment. The only piece of pleasantry in *Paradise Lost* is where
the evil spirits are described as rallying the angels upon the
success of their new invented artillery. This passage I look
upon to be the silliest in the whole poem, as being nothing
else but a string of puns, and those too very indifferent
ones.

> . . . Satan beheld their plight,
> And to his mates thus in derision called:
> O Friends, why come not on these victors proud?
> Ere while they fierce were coming, and when we,
> To entertain them fair with open front,
> And breast (what could we more?) propounded terms
> Of composition; straight they changed their minds,
> Flew off, and into strange vagaries fell,
> As they would dance: yet for a dance they seemed
> Somewhat extravagant and wild, perhaps
> For joy of offered peace; but I suppose
> If our proposals once again were heard,
> We should compel them to a quick result.
> To whom thus Belial in like gamesome mood:
> Leader, the terms we sent were terms of weight,
> Of hard contents, and full of force urged home,
> Such as we might perceive amused them all,
> And stumbled many; who receives them right,

Had need, from head to foot, well understand;
Not understood, this gift they have besides,
They show us when our foes walk not upright.
    So they among themselves in pleasant vein
Stood scoffing. . . .[6]

No. 285

[The language of *Paradise Lost*]

Saturday, January 26, 1712

> *ne quicumque deus, quicumque adhibebitur heros,*
> *regali conspectus in auro nuper et ostro,*
> *migret in obscuras humili sermone tabernas,*
> *aut, dum vitat humum, nubes et inania captet.*—Hor.[1]

Having already treated of the fable, the characters, and
sentiments in the *Paradise Lost*, we are in the last place to
consider the language, and, as the learned world is very
much divided upon Milton as to this point, I hope they will
excuse me if I appear particular in any of my opinions and
incline to those who judge the most advantageously of the
author.

    It is requisite that the language of an heroic poem should
be both perspicuous and sublime.[2] In proportion as either
of these two qualities are wanting, the language is imperfect. Perspicuity is the first and most necessary qualification, insomuch that a good-natured reader sometimes over-
looks a little slip even in the grammar or syntax where it is

6 Satan . . . scoffing *PL* VI. 607-29   **1 ne quicumque . . . captet**
Horace *Ars Poetica* 227-30: ". . . that no god, no hero, who shall be
brought upon the stage, and whom we have just beheld in royal
gold and purple, shall shift with vulgar speech into dingy hovels,
or, while shunning the ground, catch at clouds and emptiness"
2 both . . . sublime Aristotle *Poetics* 22.1

impossible for him to mistake the poet's sense. Of this kind
is that passage in Milton wherein he speaks of Satan.

> . . . God and his Son except,
> Created thing naught valued he nor shunned.[3]

And that in which he describes Adam and Eve.

> Adam the goodliest man of men since born
> His sons, the fairest of her daughters Eve.[4]

It is plain that in the former of these passages, according
to the natural syntax, the Divine Persons mentioned in the
first line are represented as created beings and that, in the
other, Adam and Eve are confounded with their sons and
daughters. Such little blemishes as these, when the thought
is great and natural, we should, with Horace,[5] impute to a
pardonable inadvertency or to the weakness of human nature, which cannot attend to each minute particular and
give the last finishing to every circumstance in so long a
work. The ancient critics, therefore, who were acted by a
spirit of candor rather than that of caviling, invented certain
figures of speech on purpose to palliate little errors of this
nature in the writings of those authors who had so many
greater beauties to atone for them.

If clearness and perspicuity were only to be consulted, the
poet would have nothing else to do but to clothe his
thoughts in the most plain and natural expressions. But
since it often happens that the most obvious phrases and
those which are used in ordinary conversation become too
familiar to the ear and contract a kind of meanness by
passing through the mouths of the vulgar, a poet should
take particular care to guard himself against idiomatic ways
of speaking. Ovid and Lucan have many poornesses of
expression upon this account, as taking up with the first
phrases that offered without putting themselves to the
trouble of looking after such as would not only have been
natural but also elevated and sublime. Milton has but few
failings in this kind, of which, however, you may see an
instance or two in the following passages.

3 **God . . . shunned** *PL* II.678-9   4 **Adam . . . Eve** *PL* IV.323-4
5 **with Horace** *Ars Poetica* 351-3

> Embryos and idiots, eremites and friars
> White, black, and grey, with all their trumpery.
> Here pilgrims roam . . .[6]
> . . . A while discourse they hold;
> No fear lest dinner cool; when thus began
> Our author . . .[7]
> Who of all ages to succeed, but feeling
> The evil on him brought by me, will curse
> My head, ill fare our ancestor impure,
> For this we may thank Adam. . . .[8]

The great masters in composition know very well that many an elegant phrase becomes improper for a poet or orator when it has been debased by common use. For this reason the works of ancient authors, which are written in dead languages, have a great advantage over those which are written in languages that are now spoken. Were there any mean phrases or idioms in Vergil and Homer, they would not shock the ear of the most delicate modern reader so much as they would have done that of an old Greek or Roman, because we never hear them pronounced in our streets or in ordinary conversation.

It is not therefore sufficient that the language of an epic poem be perspicuous unless it also be sublime. To this end it ought to deviate from the common forms and ordinary phrases of speech. The judgment of a poet very much discovers itself in shunning the common roads of expression, without falling into such ways of speech as may seem stiff and unnatural; he must not swell into a false sublime by endeavoring to avoid the other extreme. Among the Greeks, Aeschylus and sometimes Sophocles were guilty of this fault; among the Latins, Claudian and Statius; and among our own countrymen, Shakespeare and Lee. In these authors the affectation of greatness often hurts the perspicuity of the style, as in many others the endeavor after perspicuity prejudices its greatness.

Aristotle has observed[9] that the idomatic style may be avoided and the sublime formed by the following methods. First, by the use of metaphors, like those in Milton.

6 Embryos . . . roam *PL* III.474-6   7 A while . . . author *PL* V.395-7   8 Who . . . Adam *PL* X.733-6   9 Aristotle has observed *Poetics* 22

> Imparadised in one another's arms,[10]
> . . . and in his hand a reed
> Stood waving tipped with fire; . . .[11]
> The grassy clods now calved, . . .[12]

In these and several other instances, the metaphors are very bold, but beautiful. I must however observe that the metaphors are not thick sown in Milton, which always savors too much of wit; that they never clash with one another, which, as Aristotle observes,[13] turns a sentence into a kind of an enigma or riddle; and that he seldom makes use of them where the proper and natural words will do as well.

Another way of raising the language and giving it a poetical turn is to make use of the idioms of other tongues. Vergil is full of the Greek forms of speech, which the critics call Hellenisms, as Horace in his odes abounds with them much more than Vergil. I need not mention the several dialects which Homer has made use of for this end. Milton in conformity with the practice of the ancient poets and with Aristotle's rule has infused a great many Latinisms as well as Graecisms into the language of his poem, as towards the beginning of it.

> Nor did they not perceive the evil plight
> In which they were, or the fierce pains not feel;[14]
> . . . Who shall tempt with wand'ring feet
> The dark unbottomed infinite abyss
> And through the palpable obscure find out
> His uncouth way, or spread his airy flight
> Upborne with indefatigable wings
> Over the vast abrupt . . .[15]

Under this head may be reckoned the placing the adjective after the substantive, the transposition of words, the turning the adjective into a substantive, with several other foreign modes of speech which this poet has naturalized to give his verse the greater sound and throw it out of prose.

---

10 Imparadised . . . arms *PL* IV.506   **11 and in his . . . fire** *PL* VI.579-80   **12 The grassy . . . calved** *PL* VII.463   **13 as Aristotle observes** *Poetics* 22   **14 Nor did they . . . feel** *PL* I.335-6   **15 Who shall . . . abrupt** *PL* II.404-9

The third method mentioned by Aristotle is that which agrees with the genius of the Greek language more than with that of any other tongue and is therefore more used by Homer than by any other poet. I mean the lengthening of a phrase by the addition of words which may either be inserted or omitted as also by the extending or contracting of particular words by the insertion or omission of certain syllables. Milton has put in practice this method of raising his language as far as the nature of our tongue will permit, as in the passage above mentioned, "eremite," what is "hermit" in common discourse. If you observe the measure of his verse, he has with great judgment suppressed a syllable in several words and shortened those of two syllables into one, by which method, besides the above-mentioned advantage, he has given a greater variety to his numbers. But this practice is more particularly remarkable in the names of persons and of countries, as Beelzebub, Hessebon, and in many other particulars wherein he has either changed the name or made use of that which is not the most commonly known that he might the better deviate from the language of the vulgar.

The same reason recommended to him several old words which also make his poem appear the more venerable and give it a greater air of antiquity.

I must likewise take notice that there are in Milton several words of his own coining, as Cerberean, miscreated, hell-doomed, embryon atoms, and many others. If the reader is offended at this liberty in our English poet, I would recommend him to a discourse in Plutarch,[16] which shows us how frequently Homer has made use of the same liberty.

Milton, by the above-mentioned helps and by the choice of the noblest words and phrases which our tongue would afford him, has carried our language to a greater height than any of the English poets have ever done before or after him and made the sublimity of his style equal to that of his sentiments.

I have been the more particular in these observations of Milton's style because it is that part of him in which he appears the most singular. The remarks I have here made upon the practice of other poets, with my observations out

16 a discourse in Plutarch not now attributed to Plutarch

of Aristotle, will perhaps alleviate the prejudice which some have taken to his poem upon this account, though after all I must confess that I think his style, though admirable in general, is in some places too much stiffened and obscured by the frequent use of those methods which Aristotle has prescribed for the raising of it.

The redundancy of those several ways of speech which Aristotle calls foreign language[17] and with which Milton has so very much enriched and in some places darkened the language of his poem is the more proper for his use because his poem is written in blank verse. Rhyme, without any other assistance, throws the language off from prose and very often makes an indifferent phrase pass unregarded. But where the verse is not built upon rhymes, there pomp of sound and energy of expression are indispensably necessary to support the style and keep it from falling into the flatness of prose.

Those who have not a taste for this elevation of style and are apt to ridicule a poet when he departs from the common forms of expression would do well to see how Aristotle has treated an ancient author, called Euclid,[18] for his insipid mirth upon this occasion. Mr. Dryden used to call this sort of men his prose-critics.

I should under this head of the language consider Milton's numbers, in which he has made use of several elisions that are not customary among other English poets, as may be particularly observed in his cutting off the letter Y when it precedes a vowel. This, and some other innovations in the measure of his verse, has varied his numbers in such a manner as makes them incapable of satiating the ear and cloying the reader, which the same uniform measure would certainly have done, and which the perpetual returns of rhyme never fail to do in long narrative poems. I shall close these reflections upon the language of *Paradise Lost* with observing that Milton has copied after Homer rather than Vergil in the length of his periods, the copiousness of his phrases, and the running of his verses into one another.

L

17 **Aristotle . . . language** Poetics 22   18 **Aristotle . . . Euclid** Poetics 22

No. 291

[*Paradise Lost* and the art of criticism]

Saturday, February 2, 1712

> . . . *ubi plura nitent in carmine, non ego paucis*
> *offendar maculis, quas aut incuria fudit*
> *aut humana parum cavit natura* . . .—Hor.[1]

I have now considered Milton's *Paradise Lost* under those
four great heads of the fable, the characters, the sentiments,
and the language, and have shown that he excels, in general, under each of these heads. I hope that I have made
several discoveries that may appear new even to those who
are versed in critical learning. Were I indeed to choose my
readers, by whose judgment I would stand or fall, they
should not be such as are acquainted only with the French
and Italian critics but also with the ancient and moderns
who have written in either of the learned languages. Above
all, I would have them well versed in the Greek and Latin
poets, without which a man very often fancies that he un-
derstands a critic when in reality he does not comprehend
his meaning.

It is in criticism as in all other sciences and speculations:
one who brings with him any implicit notions and observations which he has made in his reading of the poets will find
his own reflections methodized and explained, and perhaps
several little hints that had passed in his mind perfected and

---

1 ubi plura . . . natura Horace *Ars Poetica* 351-3: "But when the
beauties in a poem are more in number, I shall not take offence at a
few blots which a careless hand has let drop, or human frailty has
failed to avert"

improved in the works of a good critic; whereas one who has not these previous lights is very often an utter stranger to what he reads, and apt to put a wrong interpretation upon it.

Nor is it sufficient that a man who sets up for a judge in criticism should have perused the authors above mentioned unless he has also a clear and logical head. Without this talent he is perpetually puzzled and perplexed amidst his own blunders, mistakes the sense of those he would confute, or if he chances to think right does not know how to convey his thoughts to another with clearness and perspicuity. Aristotle, who was the best critic, was also one of the best logicians that ever appeared in the world.

Mr. Locke's essay on human understanding would be thought a very odd book for a man to make himself master of who would get a reputation by critical writings, though at the same time it is very certain that an author who has not learned the art of distinguishing between words and things and of ranging his thoughts and setting them in proper lights, whatever notions he may have, will lose himself in confusion and obscurity. I might further observe that there is not a Greek or Latin critic who has not shown, even in the style of his criticisms, that he was a master of all the elegance and delicacy of his native tongue.

The truth of it is, there is nothing more absurd than for a man to set up for a critic without a good insight into all the parts of learning; whereas many of those who have endeavored to signalize themselves by works of this nature among our English writers are not only defective in the above-mentioned particulars but plainly discover by the phrases which they make use of and by their confused way of thinking that they are not acquainted with the most common and ordinary systems of arts and sciences. A few general rules extracted out of the French authors, with a certain cant of words, has sometimes set up an illiterate heavy writer for a most judicious and formidable critic.

One great mark by which you may discover a critic who has neither taste nor learning is this, that he seldom ventures to praise any passage in an author which has not been before received and applauded by the public, and that his criticism turns wholly upon little faults and errors. This part of a critic is so very easy to succeed in that we find every

ordinary reader upon the publishing of a new poem has wit
and ill-nature enough to turn several passages of it into
ridicule and very often in the right place. This Mr. Dryden
has very agreeably remarked in those two celebrated lines,

> Errors, like straws, upon the surface flow;
> He who would search for pearls, must dive below.[2]

A true critic ought to dwell rather upon excellencies than
imperfections, to discover the concealed beauties of a writer
and communicate to the world such things as are worth
their observation. The most exquisite words and finest
strokes of an author are those which very often appear the
most doubtful and exceptionable to a man who wants a
relish for polite learning, and they are these which a sour,
undistinguishing critic generally attacks with the greatest
violence. Tully observes that it is very easy to brand or fix a
mark upon what he calls *verbum ardens*,[3] or, as it may be
rendered into English, a glowing bold expression, and to
turn it into ridicule by a cold, ill-natured criticism. A little
wit is equally capable of exposing a beauty and of aggravat-
ing a fault, and though such a treatment of an author naturally produces indignation in the mind of an understanding
reader, it has however its effect among the generality of
those whose hands it falls into, the rabble of mankind being
very apt to think that everything which is laughed at with
any mixture of wit is ridiculous in itself.

Such a mirth as this is always unseasonable in a critic, as it
rather prejudices the reader than convinces him and is capable of making a beauty as well as a blemish the subject of
derision. A man who cannot write with wit on a proper
subject is dull and stupid, but one who shows it in an
improper place is as impertinent and absurd. Besides, a
man who has the gift of ridicule is very apt to find fault with
anything that gives him an opportunity of exerting his
beloved talent and very often censures a passage, not because there is any fault in it, but because he can be merry
upon it. Such kinds of pleasantry are very unfair and disin-
genuous in works of criticism, in which the greatest mas-

2 Errors . . . below *All for Love*, Prologue, ll. 25-6   3 **verbum
ardens** Marcus Tullius Cicero, *Ad Marcum Brutum Orator* 8.27

ters, both ancient and modern, have always appeared with a serious and instructive air.

As I intend in my next paper to show the defects in Milton's *Paradise Lost*, I thought fit to premise these few particulars, to the end that the reader may know I enter upon it as on a very ungrateful work and that I shall just point at the imperfections without endeavoring to inflame them with ridicule. I must also observe with Longinus[4] that the productions of a great genius, with many lapses and inadvertencies, are infinitely preferable to the works of an inferior kind of author which are scrupulously exact and conformable to all the rules of correct writing.

I shall conclude my paper with a story out of Boccalini[5] which sufficiently shows us the opinion that judicious author entertained of the sort of critics I have been here mentioning. A famous critic, says he, having gathered together all the faults of an eminent poet, made a present of them to Apollo, who received them very graciously and resolved to make the author a suitable return for the trouble he had been at in collecting them. In order to this, he set before him a sack of wheat as it had been just threshed out of the sheaf. He then bid him pick out the chaff from among the corn and lay it aside by itself. The critic applied himself to the task with great industry and pleasure, and after having made the due separation was presented by Apollo with the chaff for his pains.

L

4 **Longinus** *On the Sublime* 36   5 **Boccalini** Traiano Boccalini (1556-1613), *De' Ragguagli di Parnaso* (1612, 1613), trans. 1656

No. 297

[The faults of *Paradise Lost*]

Saturday, February 9, 1712

> . . . *velut si*
> *egregio inspersos reprehendas corpore naevos*—Hor.[1]

After what I have said in my last Saturday's paper, I shall enter on the subject of this without farther preface and remark the several defects which appear in the fable, the characters, the sentiments, and the language of Milton's *Paradise Lost*, not doubting but the reader will pardon me if I allege at the same time whatever may be said for the extenuation of such defects. The first imperfection which I shall observe in the fable is that the event of it is unhappy.

The fable of every poem is, according to Aristotle's division, either simple or implex.[2] It is called simple when there is no change of fortune in it, implex when the fortune of the chief actor changes from bad to good or from good to bad. The implex fable is thought the most perfect, I suppose because it is more proper to stir up the passions of the reader and to surprise him with a greater variety of accidents.

The implex fable is therefore of two kinds: in the first, the chief actor makes his way through a long series of dangers and difficulties till he arrives at honor and prosperity, as we see in the stories of Ulysses and Aeneas; in the second, the chief actor in the poem falls from some eminent pitch of honor and prosperity into misery and disgrace. Thus we see Adam and Eve sinking from a state of innocence and happiness into the most abject condition of sin and sorrow.

1 **velut si egregio . . . naevos** Horace *Satires* 1.6.66-7: ". . . even as you might find fault with moles spotted over a comely person"
2 **simple or implex** *Poetics* 10

The most taking tragedies among the ancients were built on this last sort of implex fable, particularly the tragedy of *Oedipus*, which proceeds upon a story, if we may believe Aristotle,[3] the most proper for tragedy that could be invented by the wit of man. I have taken some pains in a former paper to show that this kind of implex fable, wherein the event is unhappy, is more apt to affect an audience than that of the first kind, notwithstanding many excellent pieces among the ancients as well as most of those which have been written of late years in our own country are raised upon contrary plans. I must, however, own that I think this kind of fable, which is the most perfect in tragedy, is not so proper for an heroic poem.

Milton seems to have been sensible of this imperfection in his fable and has therefore endeavored to cure it by several expedients, particularly by the mortification which the great adversary of mankind meets with upon his return to the assembly of infernal spirits, as it is described in that beautiful passage of the tenth book, and likewise by the vision wherein Adam at the close of the poem sees his offspring triumphing over his great enemy and himself restored to a happier paradise than that from which he fell.

There is another objection against Milton's fable which is indeed almost the same with the former, though placed in a different light; namely, that the hero in the *Paradise Lost* is unsuccessful and by no means a match for his enemies. This gave occasion to Mr. Dryden's reflection[4] that the Devil was in reality Milton's hero. I think I have obviated this objection in my first paper. The *Paradise Lost* is an epic, narrative poem; he that looks for a hero in it searches for that which Milton never intended, or if he will needs fix the name of a hero upon any person in it, 'tis certainly the Messiah who is the hero, both in the principal action and in the episode. Paganism could not furnish out a real action for a fable greater than that of the *Iliad* or *Aeneid*, and therefore a heathen could not form a higher notion of a poem than one of that kind, which they call an heroic. Whether Milton's is not of a greater nature I will not presume to determine. It is sufficient that I show there is in the *Paradise Lost* all the

3 believe Aristotle *Poetics* 11   **4 Dryden's reflection** dedicatory epistle prefixed to translation of the *Aeneid*

greatness of plan, regularity of design, and masterly beauties which we discover in Homer and Vergil.

I must in the next place observe that Milton has interwoven in the texture of his fable some particulars which do not seem to have probability enough for an epic poem, particularly in the actions which he ascribes to Sin and Death and the picture which he draws of the Limbo of Vanity,[5] with other passages in the second book. Such allegories rather savor of the spirit of Spenser and Ariosto than of Homer and Vergil.

In the structure of his poem he has likewise admitted of too many digressions. It is finely observed by Aristotle[6] that the author of an heroic poem should seldom speak himself but throw as much of his work as he can into the mouths of those who are his principal actors. Aristotle has given no reason for this precept, but I presume it is because the mind of the reader is more awed and elevated when he hears Aeneas or Achilles speak than when Vergil or Homer talk in their own persons, besides that assuming the character of an eminent man is apt to fire the imagination and raise the ideas of the author. Tully tells us,[7] mentioning his dialogue of old age,[8] in which Cato[9] is the chief speaker, that upon a review of it he was agreeably imposed upon and fancied that it was Cato and not he himself who uttered his thoughts on that subject.

If the reader would be at the pains to see how the story of the *Iliad* and the *Aeneid* is delivered by those persons who act in it, he will be surprised to find how little in either of these poems proceeds from the authors. Milton has in the general disposition of his fable very finely observed this great rule, insomuch that there is scarce a third part of it which comes from the poet; the rest is spoken either by Adam and Eve or by some good or evil spirit who is engaged either in their destruction or defense.

From what has been here observed it appears that digressions are by no means to be allowed of in an epic poem. If the poet, even in the ordinary course of his narration, should speak as little as possible, he should certainly never let his narration sleep for the sake of any reflections of his

5 **Limbo of Vanity** *PL* III.437-97   6 **observed by Aristotle** *Poetics*
24 7 **Tully tells us** Marcus Tullius Cicero *De Amicitia* 1.4   8 **his
. . . age** *De Senectute*   9 **Cato** Marcus Porcius Cato (234-149 B.C.)

own. I have often observed with a secret admiration that the longest reflection in the *Aeneid* is in that passage of the tenth book where Turnus is represented as dressing himself in the spoils of Pallas, whom he had slain. Vergil here lets his fable stand still for the sake of the following remark: "How is the mind of man ignorant of futurity and unable to bear prosperous fortune with moderation? The time will come when Turnus shall wish that he had left the body of Pallas untouched and curse the day on which he dressed himself in these spoils."[10] As the great event of the *Aeneid* and the death of Turnus, whom Aeneas slew because he saw him adorned with the spoils of Pallas, turns upon this incident, Vergil went out of his way to make this reflection upon it, without which so small a circumstance might possibly have slipped out of his reader's memory. Lucan, who was an injudicious poet, lets drop his story very frequently for the sake of unnecessary digressions, or his *diverticula*, as a Scaliger[11] calls them. If he gives us an account of the prodigies which preceded the civil war, he declaims upon the occasion and shows how much happier it would be for man if he did not feel his evil fortune before it comes to pass and suffer not only by its real weight but by the apprehension of it. Milton's complaint of his blindness, his panegyric on marriage, his reflections on Adam and Eve's going naked, of the angels eating, and several other passages in his poem are liable to the same exception, though I must confess there is so great a beauty in these very digressions that I would not wish them out of his poem.

I have in a former paper spoken of the characters of Milton's *Paradise Lost* and declared my opinion as to the allegorical persons who are introduced in it.

If we look into the sentiments, I think they are sometimes defective under the following heads. First, as there are some of them too much pointed and some that degenerate even into puns. Of this last kind I am afraid is that in the first book where, speaking of the Pygmies, he calls them

> . . . that small infantry
> Warred on by cranes: . . .[12]

Another blemish which appears in some of his thoughts

---

10 "How is the mind . . . these spoils" *Aeneid* 10.501-5
11 **Scaliger** Julius Caesar Scaliger (1484-1558), *Poetices* 6.6 (Lyons, 1561, p. 326)   **12** **That small . . . cranes** *PL* I.575-6

is his frequent allusion to the heathen fables, which are not certainly of a piece with the divine subject of which he treats. I do not find fault with these allusions where the poet himself represents them as fabulous, as he does in some places, but where he mentions them as truths and matters of fact. The limits of my paper will not give me leave to be particular in instances of this kind; the reader will easily remark them in his perusal of the poem.

A third fault in his sentiments is an unnecessary ostentation of learning which likewise occurs very frequently. It is certain that both Homer and Vergil were masters of all the learning of their times, but it shows itself in their works after an indirect and concealed manner. Milton seems ambitious of letting us know, by his excursions on free will and predestination and his many glances upon history, astronomy, geography, and the like, as well as by the terms and the phrases he sometimes makes use of, that he was acquainted with the whole circle of arts and sciences.

If, in the last place, we consider the language of this great poet, we must allow what I have hinted in a former paper, that it is too much labored and sometimes obscured by old words, transpositions, and foreign idioms. Seneca's objection to the style of a great author, *Riget eius oratio, nihil in eâ placidum, nihil lene,*[13] is what many critics make to Milton. As I cannot wholly refute it, so I have already apologized for it in another paper; to which I may further add that Milton's sentiments and ideas were so wonderfully sublime that it would have been impossible for him to have represented them in their full strength and beauty without having recourse to these foreign assistances. Our language sunk under him and was unequal to that greatness of soul which furnished him with such glorious conceptions.

A second fault in his language is that he often affects a kind of jingle in his words, as in the following passages, and many others:

> That brought into this world a world of woe[14]
> . . . begirt th' Almighty throne

13 **Seneca's objection . . . nihil lene** "Seneca the Elder, *Controversies* 7.4.8 (altered). His manner of speech is stiff; there is nothing gentle or easy in it. The 'great author' is Calvus, who waged with Cicero a very unequal contest for supremacy among Roman orators" (Bond, III, 62n) 14 **That brought . . . woe** *PL* IX.11

Beseeching or besieging. . . .[15]
Which tempted our attempt . . .[16]
At one slight bound high overleaped all bound[17]

I know there are figures for this kind of speech, that some of the greatest ancients have been guilty of it, and that Aristotle himself has given it a place in his *Rhetoric* [18] among the beauties of that art. But as it is in itself poor and trifling, it is I think at present universally exploded by all the masters of polite writing.

The last fault which I shall take notice of in Milton's style is the frequent use of what the learned call technical words or terms of art. It is one of the greatest beauties of poetry to make hard things intelligible and deliver what is abstruse in itself in such easy language as may be understood by ordinary readers; besides that the knowledge of a poet should rather seem born with him, or inspired, than drawn from books and systems. I have often wondered how Mr. Dryden could translate a passage of Vergil after the following manner.

Tack to the larboard, and stand off to sea:
Veer starboard sea and land. . . .[19]

Milton makes use of "larboard"[20] in the same manner. When he is upon building he mentions Doric pillars, pilasters, cornice, frieze, architrave. When he talks of heavenly bodies you meet with ecliptic and eccentric, the trepidation, stars dropping from the zenith, rays culminating from the equator. To which might be added many instances of the like kind in several other arts and sciences.

I shall in my next Saturday's paper give an account of the many particular beauties in Milton which would have been too long to insert under those general heads I have already treated of, and with which I intend to conclude this piece of criticism.

L

15 begirt . . . besieging *PL* V.868-9   16 Which . . . attempt *PL* I.642   17 At one . . . bound *PL* IV.181   18 Aristotle . . . Rhetoric 3.11   19 Tack . . . land trans. *Aeneid* 3.526-7   20 Milton . . . "larboard" *PL* 11.1019

TASTE

No. 409

[The nature of taste in literary criticism]

Thursday, June 19, 1712

. . . musaeo contingens cuncta lepore.—Lucr.[1]

Gracián[2] very often recommends the fine taste as the utmost perfection of an accomplished man. As this word arises very often in conversation, I shall endeavor to give some account of it and to lay down rules how we may know whether we are possessed of it and how we may acquire that fine taste of writing which is so much talked of among the polite world.

Most languages make use of this metaphor to express that faculty of the mind which distinguishes all the most concealed faults and nicest perfections in writing. We may be sure this metaphor would not have been so general in all tongues had there not been a very great conformity between that mental taste which is the subject of this paper and that sensitive taste which gives us a relish of every different flavor that affects the palate. Accordingly we find that there are as many degrees of refinement in the intellectual faculty as in the sense which is marked out by this common denomination.

1 musaeo . . . lepore Lucretius, *De Rerum Natura*, 1.934: ". . . as I touch all with the Muses' grace" **2 Gracián** Baltasar Gracián y Morales (1601-1658), Spanish literary theorist and moral philosopher

I knew a person who possessed the one in so great a perfection that after having tasted ten different kinds of tea he would distinguish, without seeing the color of it, the particular sort which was offered him, and not only so, but any two sorts of them that were mixed together in an equal proportion; nay, he has carried the experiment so far as upon tasting the composition of three different sorts to name the parcels from whence the three several ingredients were taken. A man of a fine taste in writing will discern after the same manner not only the general beauties and imperfections of an author but discover the several ways of thinking and expressing himself which diversify him from all other authors, with the several foreign infusions of thought and language and the particular authors from whom they were borrowed.

After having thus far explained what is generally meant by a fine taste in writing and shown the propriety of the metaphor which is used on this occasion, I think I may define it to be that faculty of the soul which discerns the beauties of an author with pleasure and the imperfections with dislike. If a man would know whether he is possessed of this faculty, I would have him read over the celebrated works of antiquity, which have stood the test of so many different ages and countries, or those works among the moderns which have the sanction of the politer part of our contemporaries. If upon the perusal of such writings he does not find himself delighted in an extraordinary manner or if upon reading the admired passages in such authors he finds a coldness and indifference in his thoughts, he ought to conclude not (as is too usual among tasteless readers) that the author has not those perfections which have been admired in him but that he himself wants the faculty of discovering them.

He should, in the second place, be very careful to observe whether he tastes the distinguishing perfections or, if I may be allowed to call them so, the specific qualities of the author whom he peruses, whether he is particularly pleased with Livy for his manner of telling a story, with Sallust for his entering into those internal principles of action which arise from the characters and manners of the persons he describes, or with Tacitus for his displaying those outward motives of safety and interest which give birth to the whole series of transactions which he relates.

He may likewise consider how differently he is affected by the same thought which presents itself in a great writer from what he is when he finds it delivered by a person of an ordinary genius; for there is as much difference in apprehending a thought clothed in Cicero's language and that of a common author as in seeing an object by the light of a taper or by the light of the sun.

It is very difficult to lay down rules for the acquirement of such a taste as that I am here speaking of. The faculty must in some degree be born with us, and it very often happens that those who have other qualities in perfection are wholly void of this. One of the most eminent mathematicians of the age has assured me that the greatest pleasure he took in reading Vergil was in examining Aeneas his voyage by the map, as I question not but many a modern compiler of history would be delighted with little more in that divine author than in the bare matters of fact.

But notwithstanding this faculty must in some measure be born with us, there are several methods for cultivating and improving it and without which it will be very uncertain and of little use to the person that possesses it. The most natural method for this purpose is to be conversant among the writings of the most polite authors. A man who has any relish for fine writing either discovers new beauties or receives stronger impressions from the masterly strokes of a great author every time he peruses him, besides that he naturally wears himself into the same manner of speaking and thinking.

Conversation with men of a polite genius is another method for improving our natural taste. It is impossible for a man of the greatest parts to consider anything in its whole extent and in all its variety of lights. Every man, besides those general observations which are to be made upon an author, forms several reflections that are peculiar to his own manner of thinking, so that conversation will naturally furnish us with hints which we did not attend to and make us enjoy other men's parts and reflections as well as our own. This is the best reason I can give for the observation which several have made that men of great genius in the same way of writing seldom rise up singly, but at certain periods of time appear together and in a body as they did at Rome in the reign of Augustus and in Greece about the age of Socrates. I cannot think that either Corneille, Racine, Moliere,

Boileau, La Fontaine, Bruyère, Bossu, or the Daciers would have written so well as they have done had they not been friends and contemporaries.

It is likewise necessary for a man who would form to himself a finished taste of good writing to be well versed in the works of the best critics both ancient and modern. I must confess that I could wish there were authors of this kind who, beside the mechanical rules which a man of very little taste may discourse upon, would enter into the very spirit and soul of fine writing and show us the several sources of that pleasure which rises in the mind upon the perusal of a noble work. Thus although in poetry it be absolutely necessary that the unities of time, place, and action with other points of the same nature should be thoroughly explained and understood, there is still something more essential to the art, something that elevates and astonishes the fancy and gives a greatness of mind to the reader, which few of the critics besides Longinus have considered.

Our general taste in England is for epigram, turns of wit, and forced conceits which have no manner of influence either for the bettering or enlarging the mind of him who reads them and have been carefully avoided by the greatest writers both among the ancients and moderns. I have endeavored in several of my speculations to banish this Gothic taste which has taken possession among us. I entertained the town for a week together with an essay upon wit in which I endeavored to detect several of those false kinds which have been admired in the different ages of the world and at the same time to show wherein the nature of true wit consists. I afterwards gave an instance of the great force which lies in a natural simplicity of thought to affect the mind of the reader from such vulgar pieces as have little else besides this single qualification to recommend them. I have likewise examined the works of the greatest poet which our nation or perhaps any other has produced and particularized most of those rational and manly beauties which give a value to that divine work. I shall next Saturday enter upon an essay on the pleasures of the imagination, which, though it shall consider that subject at large, will perhaps suggest to the reader what it is that gives a beauty to many passages of the finest writers both in prose and verse. As an undertaking of this nature is entirely new, I question not but it will be received with candor.

O

THE PLEASURES OF THE IMAGINATION

No. 411

[Introductory]

Saturday, June 21, 1712

> *avia Pieridum peragro loca nullius ante*
> *trita solo. :urat integros accedere fontis*
> *atque haurire . . .*—Lucr.[1]

Our sight is the most perfect and most delightful of all our senses. It fills the mind with the largest variety of ideas, converses with its objects at the greatest distance, and continues the longest in action without being tired or satiated with its proper enjoyments. The sense of feeling can indeed give us a notion of extension, shape, and all other ideas that enter at the eye, except colors; but at the same time it is very much straitened and confined in its operations to the number, bulk, and distance of its particular objects. Our sight therefore seems designed to supply all these defects, and may be considered as a more delicate and diffusive kind of touch that spreads itself over an infinite multitude of bodies, comprehends the largest figures, and brings into our reach some of the most remote parts of the universe.

1 **avia Pieridum . . . haurire** Lucretius, *De Rerum Natura*, 1.926-8: ". . . in lively thought I traverse pathless tracts of the Pierides never yet trodden by any foot. I love to approach virgin springs and there to drink . . . "

It is this sense which furnishes the imagination with its ideas; so that by the pleasures of the imagination or fancy (which I shall use promiscuously) I here mean such as arise from visible objects, either when we have them actually in our view, or when we call up their ideas into our minds by paintings, statues, descriptions, or any the like occasion. We cannot indeed have a single image in the fancy that did not make its first entrance through the sight. But we have the power of retaining, altering, and compounding those images which we have once received into all the varieties of picture and vision that are most agreeable to the imagination; for by this faculty a man in a dungeon is capable of entertaining himself with scenes and landscapes more beautiful than any that can be found in the whole compass of nature.

There are few words in the English language which are employed in a more loose and uncircumscribed sense than those of the fancy and the imagination. I therefore thought it necessary to fix and determine the notion of these two words, as I intend to make use of them in the thread of my following speculations, that the reader may conceive rightly what is the subject which I proceed upon. I must therefore desire him to remember that by the pleasures of the imagination I mean only such pleasures as arise originally from sight, and that I divide these pleasures into two kinds: my design being first of all to discourse of those primary pleasures of the imagination which entirely proceed from such objects as are present to the eye; and in the next place to speak of those secondary pleasures of the imagination which flow from the ideas of visible objects when the objects are not actually before the eye, but are called up into our memories or formed into agreeable visions of things that are either absent or fictitious.

The pleasures of the imagination, taken in their full extent, are not so gross as those of sense, nor so refined as those of the understanding. The last are indeed more preferable, because they are founded on some new knowledge or improvement in the mind of man; yet it must be confessed that those of the imagination are as great and as transporting as the other. A beautiful prospect delights the soul as much as a demonstration, and a description in Homer has charmed more readers than a chapter in Aristotle. Besides, the pleasures of the imagination have this advantage above those of the understanding, that they are more obvious and more easy to be acquired. It is but opening the eye and the scene enters. The colors paint themselves on the fancy with very little attention of thought or application of mind in the beholder. We are struck, we know not how, with the symmetry of anything we see, and immediately assent to the beauty of an object, without enquiring into the particular causes and occasions of it.

A man of a polite imagination is let into a great many pleasures that the vulgar are not capable of receiving. He can converse with a picture and find an agreeable companion in a statue. He meets with a secret refreshment in a description and often feels a greater satisfaction in the prospect of fields and meadows than another does in the possession. It gives him indeed a kind of property in everything he sees and makes the most rude, uncultivated parts of nature administer to his pleasures, so that he looks upon the world, as it were, in another light and discovers in it a multitude of charms that conceal themselves from the generality of mankind.

There are, indeed, but very few who know how to be idle and innocent or have a relish of any pleasures that are not criminal; every diversion they take is at the expense of some one virtue or another, and their very first step out of business is into vice or folly. A man should endeavor, therefore, to make the sphere of his innocent pleasures as wide as possible, that he may retire into them with safety and find in them such a satisfaction as a wise man would not blush to take. Of this nature are those of the imagination, which do not require such a bent of thought as is necessary to our more serious employments, nor, at the same time, suffer the mind to sink into that negligence and remissness which are apt to accompany our more sensual delights, but, like a gentle exercise to the faculties, awaken them from sloth and idleness without putting them upon any labor or difficulty.

We might here add that the pleasures of the fancy are more conducive to health than those of the understanding, which are worked out by dint of thinking and attended with too violent a labor of the brain. Delightful scenes, whether in nature, painting, or poetry, have a kindly influence on the body as well as the mind, and not only serve to clear and brighten the imagination, but are able to disperse grief and melancholy and to set the animal spirits in pleasing and agreeable motions. For this reason Sir Francis Bacon, in his essay upon health, has not thought it improper to prescribe to his reader a poem or a prospect where he particularly dissuades him from knotty and subtle disquisitions, and advises him to pursue studies that fill the mind with splendid and illustrious objects, as histories, fables, and contemplations of nature.

I have in this paper, by way of introduction, settled the notion of those pleasures of the imagination which are the subject of my present undertaking and endeavored, by several considerations, to recommend to my reader the pursuit of those pleasures. I shall, in my next paper, examine the several sources from whence these pleasures are derived.

O

No. 412

[Pleasures of the imagination derived from the great, the uncommon, and the beautiful]

Monday, June 23, 1712

. . . divisum sic breve fiet opus.—Mart.[1]

I shall first consider those pleasures of the imagination that arise from the actual view and survey of outward objects, and these, I think, all proceed from the sight of what is great, uncommon, or beautiful. There may, indeed, be something

1 **divisum . . . opus** Martial *Epigrams* 4.82.8: ". . . divided, the work will thus become brief"

so terrible or offensive that the horror or loathsomeness of an object may overbear the pleasure that results from its greatness, novelty, or beauty. But still there will be such a mixture of delight in the very disgust it gives us, as any of these three qualifications are most conspicuous and prevailing.

By greatness I do not only mean the bulk of any single object, but the largeness of a whole view considered as one entire piece. Such are the prospects of an open champian[2] country, a vast uncultivated desert of huge heaps of mountains, high rocks and precipices, or a wide expanse of waters, where we are not struck with the novelty or beauty of the sight, but with that rude kind of magnificence which appears in many of these stupendous works of nature. Our imagination loves to be filled with an object or to grasp at anything that is too big for its capacity. We are flung into a pleasing astonishment at such unbounded views and feel a delightful stillness and amazement in the soul at the apprehension of them. The mind of man naturally hates everything that looks like a restraint upon it and is apt to fancy itself under a sort of confinement when the sight is pent up in a narrow compass and shortened on every side by the neighborhood of walls or mountains. On the contrary, a spacious horizon is an image of liberty where the eye has room to range abroad, to expatiate at large on the immensity of its views, and to lose itself amidst the variety of objects that offer themselves to its observation. Such wide and undetermined prospects are as pleasing to the fancy as the speculations of eternity or infinitude are to the understanding. But if there be a beauty or uncommonness joined with this grandeur, as in a troubled ocean, a heaven adorned with stars and meteors, or a spacious landscape cut out into rivers, woods, rocks, and meadows, the pleasure still grows upon us, as it arises from more than a single principle.

Everything that is new or uncommon raises a pleasure in the imagination because it fills the soul with an agreeable surprise, gratifies its curiosity, and gives it an idea of which it was not before possessed. We are indeed so often conversant with one set of objects and tired out with so many repeated shows of the same things that whatever is new or uncommon contributes a little to vary human life and to

2 **champian**   champaign; flat, open country

divert our minds, for a while, with the strangeness of its appearance. It serves us for a kind of refreshment and takes off from that satiety we are apt to complain of in our usual and ordinary entertainments. It is this that bestows charms on a monster and makes even the imperfections of nature to please us. It is this that recommends variety, where the mind is every instant called off to something new and the attention not suffered to dwell too long and waste itself on any particular object. It is this, likewise, that improves what is great or beautiful and makes it afford the mind a double entertainment. Groves, fields, and meadows are at any season of the year pleasant to look upon, but never so much as in the opening of the spring, when they are all new and fresh with their first gloss upon them and not yet too much accustomed and familiar to the eye. For this reason there is nothing that more enlivens a prospect than rivers, jetteaus,[3] or falls of water, where the scene is perpetually shifting and entertaining the sight every moment with something that is new. We are quickly tired with looking upon hills and valleys, where everything continues fixed and settled in the same place and posture, but find our thoughts a little agitated and relieved at the sight of such objects as are ever in motion and sliding away from beneath the eye of the beholder.

But there is nothing that makes its way more directly to the soul than beauty, which immediately diffuses a secret satisfaction and complacency through the imagination and gives a finishing to anything that is great or uncommon. The very first discovery of it strikes the mind with an inward joy and spreads a cheerfulness and delight through all its faculties. There is not perhaps any real beauty or deformity more in one piece of matter than another, because we might have been so made that whatsoever now appears loathsome to us might have shown itself agreeable. But we find by experience that there are several modifications of matter which the mind, without any previous consideration, pronounces at first sight beautiful or deformed. Thus we see that every different species of sensible creatures has its different notions of beauty and that each of them is most affected with the beauties of its own kind. This is nowhere more remarkable than in birds of the same shape and pro-

3 jetteaus   "jets d'eau", fountains

portion, where we often see the male determined in his
courtship by the single grain or tincture of a feather and
never discovering any charms but in the color of its own
species.

Scit thalamo servare fidem, sanctasque veretur
Connubii leges; non illum in pectore candor
Sollicitat niveus; neque pravum accendit amorem
Splendida lanugo, vel honesta in vertice crista,
Purpureusve nitor pennarum; ast agmina late
Foeminea explorat cautus, maculasque requirit
Cognatas, paribusque interlita corpora guttis:
Ni faceret, pictis sylvam circum undique monstris
Confusam aspiceres vulgo, partusque biformes,
Et genus ambiguum, & Veneris monumenta nefandae.
　　Hinc merula in nigro se oblectat nigra marito,
Hinc socium lasciva petit Philomela canorum,
Agnoscitque pares sonitus, hinc Noctua tetram
Canitiem alarum, & Glaucos miratur ocellos.
Nempe sibi semper constat. crescitque quotannis
Lucida progenies, castos confessa parentes;
Dum virides inter saltus lucosque sonoros
Vere novo exultat, plumasque decora Juventus
Explicat ad solem, patriisque coloribus ardet.[4]

4 Scit thalamo . . . ardet These lines are Addison's. A translation
appears in the 1767 edition of *The Spectator*, as follows:
　　　The feathered husband, to his partner true,
　　　Preserves connubial rites inviolate.
　　　With cold indifferent charm he sees,
　　　The milky whiteness of the stately neck,
　　　The shining down, proud crest, and purple wings:
　　　But cautious with a searching eye explores
　　　The female tribes, his proper mate to find,
　　　With kindred colors marked: Did he not so,
　　　The grove with painted monsters would abound,
　　　Th' ambiguous product of unnatural love.
　　　The blackbird hence selects her sooty spouse;
　　　The nightingale her musical compeer,
　　　Lured by the well-known voice: the bird of night,
　　　Smit with his dusky wings and greenish eyes,
　　　Wooes his dun paramour. The beauteous race
　　　Speak the chaste loves of their progenitors;
　　　When, by the spring invited, they exult
　　　In woods and fields, and to the sun unfold
　　　Their plumes, that with paternal colors glow

There is a second kind of beauty that we find in the several products of art and nature, which does not work in the imagination with that warmth and violence as the beauty that appears in our proper species, but is apt however to raise in us a secret delight and a kind of fondness for the places or objects in which we discover it. This consists either in the gaiety or variety of colors, in the symmetry and proportion of parts, in the arrangement and disposition of bodies, or in a just mixture and concurrence of all together. Among these several kinds of beauty the eye takes most delight in colors. We nowhere meet with a more glorious or pleasing show in nature than what appears in the heavens at the rising and setting of the sun, which is wholly made up of those different stains of light that show themselves in clouds of a different situation. For this reason we find the poets, who are always addressing themselves to the imagination, borrowing more of their epithets from colors than from any other topic.

As the fancy delights in everything that is great, strange, or beautiful, and is still more pleased the more it finds of these perfections in the same object, so is it capable of receiving a new satisfaction by the assistance of another sense. Thus any continued sound, as the music of birds or a fall of water, awakens every moment the mind of the beholder and makes him more attentive to the several beauties of the place that lie before him. Thus if there arises a fragrancy of smells or perfumes, they heighten the pleasures of the imagination and make even the colors and verdure of the landscape appear more agreeable; for the ideas of both senses recommend each other and are pleasanter together than when they enter the mind separately, as the different colors of a picture, when they are well disposed, set off one another and receive an additional beauty from the advantage of their situation.

O

No. 413

[Divine purpose responsible for the pleasures of the imagination]

Tuesday, June 24, 1712

. . . causa latet, vis est notissima . . .—Ovid[1]

Though in yesterday's paper we considered how everything that is great, new, or beautiful is apt to affect the imagination with pleasure, we must own that it is impossible for us to assign the necessary cause of this pleasure, because we know neither the nature of an idea nor the substance of a human soul which might help us to discover the conformity or disagreeableness of the one to the other. And therefore, for want of such a light, all that we can do in speculations of this kind is to reflect on those operations of the soul that are most agreeable and to range under their proper heads what is pleasing or displeasing to the mind without being able to trace out the several necessary causes from whence the pleasure or displeasure arises.

Final causes lie more bare and open to our observation, as there are often a greater variety that belong to the same effect; and these, though they are not altogether so satisfactory, are generally more useful than the other, as they give us greater occasion of admiring the goodness and wisdom of the First Contriver.

One of the final causes of our delight in anything that is great may be this. The Supreme Author of our being has so formed the soul of man that nothing but himself can be its last, adequate, and proper happiness. Because, therefore, a

1 **causa . . . notissima** Ovid *Metamorphoses* 4.287: "The cause is hidden; but the enfeebling power is well known"

great part of our happiness must arise from the contemplation of his being, that he might give our souls a just relish of
such a contemplation, he has made them naturally delight
in the apprehension of what is great or unlimited. Our
admiration, which is a very pleasing motion of the mind,
immediately rises at the consideration of any object that
takes up a great deal of room in the fancy and, by consequence, will improve into the highest pitch of astonishment
and devotion when we contemplate his nature, that is
neither circumscribed by time nor place nor to be comprehended by the largest capacity of a created being.

He has annexed a secret pleasure to the idea of any thing
that is new or uncommon that he might encourage us in the
pursuit after knowledge and engage us to search into the
wonders of his creation; for every new idea brings such a
pleasure along with it as rewards any pains we have taken in
its acquisition and consequently serves as a motive to put us
upon fresh discoveries.

He has made everything that is beautiful in our own
species pleasant, that all creatures might be tempted to
multiply their kind and fill the world with inhabitants; for
'tis very remarkable that wherever nature is crossed in the
production of a monster (the result of any unnatural mixture) the breed is incapable of propagating its likeness and
of founding a new order of creatures, so that unless all
animals were allured by the beauty of their own species,
generation would be at an end and the earth unpeopled.

In the last place, he has made everything that is beautiful
in all other objects pleasant, or rather has made so many
objects appear beautiful, that he might render the whole
creation more gay and delightful. He has given almost everything about us the power of raising an agreeable idea in
the imagination, so that it is impossible for us to behold his
works with coldness or indifference and to survey so many
beauties without a secret satisfaction and complacency.
Things would make but a poor appearance to the eye if we
saw them only in their proper figures and motions. And
what reason can we assign for their exciting in us many of
those ideas which are different from anything that exists in
the objects themselves (for such are light and colors) were it
not to add supernumerary ornaments to the universe and
make it more agreeable to the imagination? We are every-

where entertained with pleasing shows and apparitions; we discover imaginary glories in the heavens and in the earth, and see some of this visionary beauty poured out upon the whole creation; but what a rough, unsightly sketch of nature should we be entertained with did all her coloring disappear and the several distinctions of light and shade vanish? In short, our souls are at present delightfully lost and bewildered in a pleasing delusion, and we walk about like the enchanted hero of a romance that sees beautiful castles, woods, and meadows and at the same time hears the warbling of birds and the purling of streams; but upon the finishing of some secret spell the fantastic scene breaks up, and the disconsolate knight finds himself on a barren heath or in a solitary desert. It is not improbable that something like this may be the state of the soul after its first separation, in respect of the images it will receive from matter, though indeed the ideas of colors are so pleasing and beautiful in the imagination that it is possible the soul will not be deprived of them, but perhaps find them excited by some other occasional cause as they are at present by the different impressions of subtle matter on the organ of sight.

I have here supposed that my reader is acquainted with that great modern discovery which is at present universally acknowledged by all the enquirers into natural philosophy: namely, that light and colors, as apprehended by the imagination, are only ideas in the mind and not qualities that have any existence in matter. As this is a truth that has been proved incontestably by many modern philosophers and is indeed one of the finest speculations in that science, if the English reader would see the notion explained at large, he may find it in the eighth chapter of the second book of Mr. Locke's essay[2] on human understanding.

O

2 **Locke's essay** *Essay Concerning Human Understanding* (1690)

No. 414

[Nature and art as sources of the pleasures of the imagination]

Wednesday, June 25, 1712

> . . . *alterius sic*
> *altera poscit opem res et coniurat amice*—Hor.[1]

If we consider the works of nature and art as they are qualified to entertain the imagination, we shall find the last very defective in comparison of the former; for though they may sometimes appear as beautiful or strange, they can have nothing in them of that vastness and immensity which afford so great an entertainment to the mind of the beholder. The one may be as polite and delicate as the other but can never show herself so august and magnificent in the design. There is something more bold and masterly in the rough careless strokes of nature than in the nice touches and embellishments of art. The beauties of the most stately garden or palace lie in a narrow compass, the imagination immediately runs them over and requires something else to gratify her; but in the wide fields of nature, the sight wanders up and down without confinement and is fed with an infinite variety of images without any certain stint or number. For this reason we always find the poet in love with a country life, where nature appears in the greatest perfection and furnishes out all those scenes that are most apt to delight the imagination.

1 alterius . . . amice Horace *Ars Poetica* 410-11: ". . . so truly does each [study and native ability] claim the other's aid, and make with it a friendly league"

scriptorum chorus omnis amat nemus et fugit urbem—
                                                    Hor.[2]

at secura quies et nescia fallere vita,
dives opum variarum, at latis otia fundis
(speluncae vivique lacus et frigida Tempe
mugitusque boum mollesque sub arbore somni)—Verg.[3]

But though there are several of these wild scenes that are
more delightful than any artificial shows, yet we find the
works of nature still more pleasant the more they resemble
those of art; for in this case our pleasure arises from a double
principle, from the agreeableness of the objects to the eye
and from their similitude to other objects. We are pleased as
well with comparing their beauties as with surveying them
and can represent them to our minds either as copies or
originals. Hence it is that we take delight in a prospect
which is well laid out and diversified with fields and
meadows, woods and rivers, in those accidental landscapes
of trees, clouds, and cities that are sometimes found in the
veins of marble, in the curious fretwork of rocks and grot-
toes, and, in a word, in anything that hath such a variety or
regularity as may seem the effect of design in what we call
the works of chance.

If the products of nature rise in value according as they
more or less resemble those of art, we may be sure that
artificial works receive a greater advantage from their resemblance of such as are natural; because here the
similitude is not only pleasant, but the pattern more perfect.
The prettiest landscape I ever saw was one drawn on the
walls of a dark room, that stood opposite on one side to a
navigable river and on the other to a park. The experiment is
very common in optics. Here you might discover the waves
and fluctuations of the water in strong and proper colors,
with the picture of a ship entering at one end and sailing by

2 scriptorum . . . urbem Horace *Epistles* 2.2.77: "The whole chorus
of poets loves the grove and flees the town"   **3 at secura . . . somni**
Vergil *Georgics* 2.467-70: "Yet theirs is repose without care, and a
life that knows no fraud, but is rich in treasures manifold. Yea, the
ease of broad domains, caverns, and living lakes, and cool vales, the
lowing of the kine, and soft slumbers beneath the trees . . ."

degrees through the whole piece. On another there appeared the green shadows of trees waving to and fro with the wind, and herds of deer among them in miniature, leaping about upon the wall. I must confess the novelty of such a sight may be one occasion of its pleasantness to the imagination, but certainly the chief reason is its near resemblance to nature, as it does not only, like other pictures, give the color and figure but the motion of the things it represents.

We have before observed that there is generally in nature something more grand and august than what we meet with in the curiosities of art. When, therefore, we see this imitated in any measure, it gives us a nobler and more exalted kind of pleasure than what we receive from the nicer and more accurate productions of art. On this account our English gardens are not so entertaining to the fancy as those in France and Italy, where we see a large extent of ground covered over with an agreeable mixture of garden and forest which represent everywhere an artificial rudeness much more charming than that neatness and elegancy which we meet with in those of our own country. It might, indeed, be of ill consequence to the public as well as unprofitable to private persons to alienate so much ground from pasturage and the plow in many parts of a country that is so well peopled and cultivated to a far greater advantage. But why may not a whole estate be thrown into a kind of garden by frequent plantations that may turn as much to the profit as the pleasure of the owner? A marsh overgrown with willows or a mountain shaded with oaks are not only more beautiful but more beneficial than when they lie bare and unadorned. Fields of corn make a pleasant prospect, and if the walks were a little taken care of that lie between them, if the natural embroidery of the meadows were helped and improved by some small additions of art and the several rows of hedges set off by trees and flowers that the soil was capable of receiving, a man might make a pretty landscape of his own possessions.

Writers who have given us an account of China tell us the inhabitants of that country laugh at the plantations of our Europeans, which are laid out by the rule and line, because, they say, anyone may place trees in equal rows and uniform figures. They choose rather to show a genius in works of this nature and therefore always conceal the art by which they direct themselves. They have a word, it seems, in their language by which they express the particular beauty of a plantation that thus strikes the imagination at first sight without discovering what it is that has so agreeable an effect. Our British gardeners, on the contrary, instead of humoring nature, love to deviate from it as much as possible. Our trees rise in cones, globes, and pyramids. We see the marks of the scissors upon every plant and bush. I do not know whether I am singular in my opinion, but for my own part I would rather look upon a tree in all its luxuriancy and diffusion of boughs and branches than when it is thus cut and trimmed into a mathematical figure, and cannot but fancy that an orchard in flower looks infinitely more delightful than all the little labyrinths of the most finished parterre. But as our great modelers of gardens have their magazines of plants to dispose of, it is very natural for them to tear up all the beautiful plantations of fruit trees and contrive a plan that may most turn to their own profit in taking off their evergreens and the like movable plants with which their shops are plentifully stocked.

O

No. 415

[Architecture as a source of the pleasures of the imagination]

Thursday, June 26, 1712

adde tot egregias urbes operumque laborem—Verg.[1]

Having already shown how the fancy is affected by the works of nature and afterwards considered in general both

---

1 adde tot . . . laborem Vergil *Georgics* 2.155: "Think, too, of all the noble cities, the achievement of man's toil"

the works of nature and of art, how they mutually assist and complete each other in forming such scenes and prospects as are most apt to delight the mind of the beholder, I shall in this paper throw together some reflections on that particular art which has a more immediate tendency than any other to produce those primary pleasures of the imagination which have hitherto been the subject of this discourse. The art I mean is that of architecture, which I shall consider only with regard to the light in which the foregoing speculations have placed it without entering into those rules and maxims which the great masters of architecture have laid down and explained at large in numberless treaties[2] upon that subject.

Greatness in the works of architecture may be considered as relating to the bulk and body of the structure or to the manner in which it is built. As for the first, we find the ancients, especially among the Eastern nations of the world, infinitely superior to the moderns.

Not to mention the Tower of Babel, of which an old author says there were the foundations to be seen in his time which looked like a spacious mountain, what could be more noble than the walls of Babylon, its hanging gardens, and its temple to Jupiter Belus that rose a mile high by eight several stories, each story a furlong in height, and on the top of which was the Babylonian observatory? I might here, likewise, take notice of the huge rock that was cut into the figure of Semiramis,[3] with the smaller rocks that lay by it in the shape of tributary kings; the prodigious basin, or artificial lake, which took in the whole Euphrates till such time as a new canal was formed for its reception, with the several trenches through which that river was conveyed. I know there are persons who look upon some of these wonders of art as fabulous, but I cannot find any grounds for such a suspicion, unless it be that we have no such works among us at present. There were indeed many greater advantages for building in those times and in that part of the world than have been met with ever since. The earth was extremely fruitful; men lived generally on pasturage, which requires a much smaller number of hands than agriculture; there were few trades to employ the busy part of mankind and fewer

2 treaties   treatises   **3 Semiramis** legendary queen of Assyria

arts and sciences to give work to men of speculative tempers; and what is more than all the rest, the prince was absolute, so that when he went to war he put himself at the head of a whole people, as we find Semiramis leading her two millions to the field and yet overpowered by the number of her enemies. 'Tis no wonder, therefore, when she was at peace and turned her thoughts on building, that she could accomplish so great works with such a prodigious multitude of laborers. Besides that, in her climate there was small interruption of frosts and winters, which make the Northern workmen lie half the year idle. I might mention too, among the benefits of the climate, what historians say of the earth: that it sweated out a bitumen or natural kind of mortar, which is doubtless the same with that mentioned in Holy Writ as contributing to the structure of Babel: "Slime they used instead of mortar."[4]

In Egypt we still see their Pyramids, which answer to the descriptions that have been made of them, and I question not but a traveler might find out some remains of the labyrinth that covered a whole province and had a hundred temples disposed among its several quarters and divisions.

The Wall of China is one of these Eastern pieces of magnificence which makes a figure even in the map of the world, although an account of it would have been thought fabulous were not the wall itself still extant.

We are obliged to devotion for the noblest buildings that have adorned the several countries of the world. It is this that has set men at work on temples and public places of worship, not only that they might by the magnificence of the building invite the deity to reside within it, but that such stupendous works might at the same time open the mind to vast conceptions and fit it to converse with the divinity of the place; for everything that is majestic imprints an awfulness and reverence on the mind of the beholder and strikes in with the natural greatness of the soul.

In the second place, we are to consider greatness of manner in architecture, which has such force upon the imagination that a small building where it appears shall give the

4 **Slime they used . . . mortar** Genesis 11:3: ". . . and slime had they for mortar"

mind nobler ideas than one of twenty times the bulk where the manner is ordinary or little. Thus, perhaps, a man would have been more astonished with the majestic air that appeared in one of Lysippus'[5] statues of Alexander, though no bigger than life, than he might have been with Mount Athos had it been cut into the figure of the hero according to the proposal of Phidias[6] with a river in one hand and a city in the other.

Let anyone reflect on the disposition of mind he finds in himself at his first entrance into the Pantheon at Rome and how his imagination is filled with something great and amazing, and at the same time consider how little in proportion he is affected with the inside of a Gothic cathedral, though it be five times larger than the other, which can arise from nothing else but the greatness of manner in the one and the meanness in the other.

I have seen an observation on this subject in a French author which very much pleased me. It is in Monsieur Fréart's[7] *Parallel of the Ancient and Modern Architecture*. I shall give it the reader with the same terms of art which he has made use of. "I am observing," says he, "a thing which, in my opinion, is very curious, whence it proceeds that in the same quantity of superficies the one manner seems great and magnificent and the other poor and trifling. The reason is fine and uncommon. I say then that to introduce into architecture this grandeur of manner we ought so to proceed that the division of the principal members of the order may consist but of few parts, that they be all great and of a bold and ample relievo[8] and swelling, and that the eye beholding nothing little and mean, the imagination may be more vigorously touched and affected with the work that stands before it. For example, in a cornice, if the gola or cymatium[9]

---

5 Lysippus Greek sculptor (fourth century B.C.). In the first edition the name is given, presumably in error, as *Protogenes; Lysippus* appears in later editions **6 Phidias** Greek sculptor and architect (fifth century B.C.) **7 Monsieur Fréart** Roland Fréart Sieur de Chambray (d. 1676?) **8 relievo** relief, the projection of a design from a plane surface to give a solid appearance (*OED*) **9 gola or cymatium** a moulding of the cornice, the outline of which consists of a concave and convex line (*OED*)

of the corona,[10] the coping,[11] the modillions,[12] or dentelli[13] make a noble show by their graceful projections, if we see none of that ordinary confusion which is the result of those little cavities, quarter rounds of the astragal,[14] and I know not how many other intermingled particulars, which produce no effect in great and massy works and which very unprofitably take up place to the prejudice of the principal member, it is most certain that this manner will appear solemn and great—as, on the contrary, that will have but a poor and mean effect where there is a redundancy of those smaller ornaments, which divide and scatter the angles of the sight into such a multitude of rays, so pressed together that the whole will appear but a confusion."

Among all the figures in architecture there are none that have a greater air than the concave and the convex, and we find in all the ancient and modern architecture, as well in the remote parts of China as in countries nearer home, that round pillars and vaulted roofs make a great part of those buildings which are designed for pomp and magnificence. The reason I take to be, because in these figures we generally see more of the body than in those of other kinds. There are, indeed, figures of bodies where the eye may take in two thirds of the surface; but as in such bodies the sight must split upon several angles, it does not take in one uniform idea, but several ideas of the same kind. Look upon the outside of a dome, your eye half surrounds it; look up into the inside, and at one glance you have all the prospect of it, the entire concavity falls into your eye at once, the sight being as the center that collects and gathers into it the lines of the whole circumference. In a square pillar the sight often takes in but a fourth part of the surface and in a square

---

10 **corona** a member of the cornice, above the bed-moulding and below the cymatium, having a broad vertical face, usually of considerable projection (*OED*)   11 **coping** the uppermost course of masonry or brick-work in a wall, usually made of a sloping form to throw off the rain (*OED*)   12 **modillions** projecting brackets placed in series under the corona of the cornice (*OED*)   13 **dentelli** small rectangular blocks, resembling a row of teeth, under the bed-moulding of the cornice (*OED*)   14 **astragal** a small moulding, of semicircular sections, sometimes carved with leaves or beads, placed round the top or bottom of columns (*OED*)

concave must move up and down to the different sides before it is master of all the inward surface. For this reason the fancy is infinitely more struck with the view of the open air and skies that passes through an arch than what comes through a square or any other figure. The figure of the rainbow does not contribute less to its beauty than the colors, as it is very poetically described by the son of Sirach:[15] "Look upon the rainbow and praise him that made it. Very beautiful it is in its brightness; it encompasses the heavens with a glorious circle, and the hands of the Almighty have bended it."[16]

Having thus spoken of that greatness which affects the mind in architecture, I might next show the pleasure that rises in the imagination from what appears new and beautiful in this art. But as every beholder has naturally a greater taste of these two perfections in every building which offers itself to his view than of that which I have hitherto considered, I shall not trouble my reader with any reflections upon it. It is sufficient for my present purpose to observe that there is nothing in this whole art which pleases the imagination but as it is great, uncommon, or beautiful.

O

---

15 son of Sirach author of the apocryphal *Book of Sirach*
16 Look upon . . . it *Sirach* 43:11-12

No. 416

[The secondary pleasures of the imagination]

Friday, June 27, 1712

quatenus hoc simile est illi, quod mente videmus—Lucr.[1]

I at first divided the pleasures of the imagination into such as arise from objects that are actually before our eyes, or that once entered in at our eyes and are afterwards called up into the mind either barely by its own operations or on occasion of something without us, as statues or descriptions. We have already considered the first division and shall therefore enter on the other, which for distinction sake I have called the secondary pleasures of the imagination. When I say the ideas we receive from statues, descriptions, or such like occasions are the same that were once actually in our view, it must not be understood that we had once seen the very place, action, or person which are carved or described. It is sufficient that we have seen places, persons, or actions in general which bear a resemblance or at least some remote analogy with what we find represented, since it is in the power of the imagination when it is once stocked with particular ideas to enlarge, compound, and vary them at her own pleasure.

Among the different kinds of representation, statuary is the most natural and shows us something likest the object that is represented. To make use of a common instance, let

1 **quatenus . . . videmus** Lucretius, *De Rerum Natura*, 4.750: "Since this [mental image] is like that [external object]—what we see with the mind like what we see with the eye—it must come about in a like way"

one who is born blind take an image in his hands and trace out with his fingers the different furrows and impressions of the chisel, and he will easily conceive how the shape of a man or beast may be represented by it; but should he draw his hand over a picture, where all is smooth and uniform, he would never be able to imagine how the several prominencies and depressions of a human body could be shown on a plain piece of canvas that has in it no unevenness or irregularity. Description runs yet further from the things it represents than painting, for a picture bears a real resemblance to its original which letters and syllables are wholly void of. Colors speak all languages, but words are understood only by such a people or nation. For this reason, though men's necessities quickly put them on finding out speech, writing is probably of a later invention than painting. Particularly we are told that in America, when the Spaniards first arrived there, expresses were sent to the emperor of Mexico in paint and the news of his country delineated by the strokes of a pencil, which was a more natural way than that of writing, though at the same time much more imperfect because it is impossible to draw the little connections of speech or to give the picture of a conjunction or an adverb. It would be yet more strange to represent visible objects by sounds that have no ideas annexed to them and to make something like description in music. Yet it is certain there may be confused, imperfect notions of this nature raised in the imagination by an artificial composition of notes, and we find that great masters in the art are able sometimes to set their hearers in the heat and hurry of a battle, to overcast their minds with melancholy scenes and apprehensions of deaths and funerals, or to lull them into pleasing dreams of groves and Elysiums.

In all these instances, this secondary pleasure of the imagination proceeds from that action of the mind which compares the ideas arising from the original objects with the ideas we receive from the statue, picture, description, or sound that represents them. It is impossible for us to give the necessary reason why this operation of the mind is attended with so much pleasure, as I have before observed on the same occasion. But we find a great variety of entertainments derived from this single principle; for it is this that not only gives us a relish of statuary, painting, and description, but makes us delight in all the actions and arts of mimicry. It is this that makes the several kinds of wit pleasant, which consists, as I have formerly shown, in the affinity of ideas, and we may add it is this also that raises the little satisfaction we sometimes find in the different sorts of false wit, whether it consist in the affinity of letters, as in an anagram, acrostic; or of syllables, as in doggerel rhymes, echoes; or of words, as in puns, quibbles; or of a whole sentence or poem to wings and altars. The final cause, probably, of annexing pleasure to this operation of the mind was to quicken and encourage us in our searches after truth, since the distinguishing one thing from another and the right discerning betwixt our ideas depends wholly upon our comparing them together and observing the congruity or disagreement that appears among the several works of nature.

But I shall here confine myself to those pleasures of the imagination that proceed from ideas raised by words, because most of the observations that agree with descriptions are equally applicable to painting and statuary.

Words, when well chosen, have so great a force in them that a description often gives us more lively ideas than the sight of things themselves. The reader finds a scene drawn in stronger colors and painted more to life in his imagination by the help of words than by an actual survey of the scene which they describe. In this case the poet seems to get the better of nature; he takes, indeed, the landscape after her, but gives it more vigorous touches, heightens its beauty, and so enlivens the whole piece that the images which flow from the objects themselves appear weak and faint in comparison of those that come from the expressions. The reason, probably, may be because in the survey of any object we have only so much of it painted on the imagination as comes in at the eye, but in its description the poet gives us as free a view of it as he pleases and discovers to us several parts that either we did not attend to or that lay out of our sight when we first beheld it. As we look on any object, our idea of it is, perhaps, made up of two or three simple ideas; but when the poet represents it, he may either give us a more complex idea of it or only raise in us such ideas as are most apt to affect the imagination.

It may be here worth our while to examine how it comes to

pass that several readers who are all acquainted with the same language and know the meaning of the words they read should nevertheless have a different relish of the same descriptions. We find one transported with a passage which another runs over with coldness and indifference or finding the representation extremely natural where another can perceive nothing of likeness and conformity. This different taste must proceed either from the perfection of imagination in one more than another or from the different ideas that several readers affix to the same words, for to have a true relish and form a right judgment of a description a man should be born with a good imagination and must have well weighed the force and energy that lie in the several words of a language so as to be able to distinguish which are most significant and expressive of their proper ideas and what additional strength and beauty they are capable of receiving from conjunction with others. The fancy must be warm, to retain the print of those images it hath received from outward objects, and the judgment discerning, to know what expressions are most proper to clothe and adorn them to the best advantage. A man who is deficient in either of these respects, though he may receive the general notion of a description, can never see distinctly all its particular beauties, as a person with a weak sight may have the confused prospect of a place that lies before him without entering into its several parts or discerning the variety of its colors in their full glory and perfection.

O

No. 417

[Pleasures of the imagination arising from the association of ideas]

Saturday, June 28, 1712

> *Quem tu, Melpomene, semel*
>   *nascentem placido lumine videris,*
> *illum non labor Isthmius*
>   *clarabit pugilem, non equus impiger, etc.*
> ....
>   *sed quae Tibur aquae fertile praefluunt,*
> *et spissae nemorum comae*
>   *fingent Aeolio carmine nobilem.*—Hor.[1]

We may observe that any single circumstance of what we have formerly seen often raises up a whole scene of imagery and awakens a thousand ideas that before slept in the imagination. Such a particular smell or color is able to fill the mind on a sudden with the picture of the fields or gardens where we first met with it and to bring up into view all the variety of images that once attended it. Our imagination takes the hint and leads us unexpectedly into cities or theaters, plains or meadows. We may further observe, when the fancy thus reflects on the scenes that have passed in it formerly, those which were at first pleasant to behold appear more so upon reflection and that the memory height-

---

1 Quem tu . . . nobilem Horace *Odes* 4.3.1-4, 10-12: "Whom thou, Melpomene, hast once beheld with favoring gaze at his natal hour, him no Isthmian toil shall make a famous boxer, no impetuous steed . . . but the waters that flow past fertile Tibur and the dense leafage of the groves shall make him famous for Aeolian song"

ens the delightfulness of the original. A Cartesian[2] would account for both these instances in the following manner.

The set of ideas which we received from such a prospect or garden, having entered the mind at the same time, have a set of traces belonging to them in the brain, bordering very near upon one another. When, therefore, any one of these ideas arises in the imagination and consequently dispatches a flow of animal spirits to its proper trace, these spirits, in the violence of their motion, run not only into the trace to which they were more particularly directed, but into several of those that lie about it. By this means they awaken other ideas of the same set, which immediately determine a new dispatch of spirits that in the same manner open other neighboring traces, till at last the whole set of them is blown up and the whole prospect or garden flourishes in the imagination. But because the pleasure we received from these places far surmounted and overcame the little disagreeableness we found in them, for this reason there was at first a wider passage worn in the pleasure traces and, on the contrary, so narrow a one in those that belonged to the disagreeable ideas that they were quickly stopped up and rendered incapable of receiving any animal spirits and consequently of exciting any unpleasant ideas in the memory.

It would be in vain to inquire whether the power of imagining things strongly proceeds from any greater perfection in the soul or from any nicer texture in the brain of one man than of another. But this is certain, that a noble writer should be born with this faculty in its full strength and vigor so as to be able to receive lively ideas from outward objects, to retain them long, and to range them together, upon occasion, in such figures and representations as are most likely to hit the fancy of the reader. A poet should take as much pains in forming his imagination as a philosopher in cultivating his understanding. He must gain a due relish of the works of nature and be thoroughly conversant in the various scenery of a country life.

When he is stored with country images, if he would go beyond pastoral and the lower kinds of poetry, he ought to acquaint himself with the pomp and magnificence of courts.

2 Cartesian follower of the French philosopher René Descartes (1596-1650)

He should be very well versed in everything that is noble and stately in the productions of art, whether it appear in painting or statuary, in the great works of architecture that are in their present glory, or in the ruins of those that flourished in former ages.

Such advantages as these help to open a man's thoughts and to enlarge his imagination and will therefore have their influence on all kinds of writing if the author knows how to make right use of them. And among those of the learned languages that excel in this talent the most perfect in their several kinds are perhaps Homer, Vergil, and Ovid. The first strikes the imagination wonderfully with what is great, the second with what is beautiful, and the last with what is strange. Reading the *Iliad* is like traveling through a country uninhabited, where the fancy is entertained with a thousand savage prospects of vast deserts, wide uncultivated marshes, huge forests, misshapen rocks and precipices. On the contrary, the *Aeneid* is like a well-ordered garden where it is impossible to find out any part unadorned or to cast our eyes upon a single spot that does not produce some beautiful plant or flower. But when we are in the *Metamorphoses* we are walking on enchanted ground and see nothing but scenes of magic lying round us.

Homer is in his province when he is describing a battle or a multitude, a hero or a god. Vergil is never better pleased than when he is in his Elysium or copying out an entertaining picture. Homer's epithets generally mark out what is great, Vergil's what is agreeable. Nothing can be more magnificent than the figure that Jupiter makes in the first *Iliad* nor more charming than that of Venus in the first *Aeneid*.

$$\text{Ἦ καὶ κυανέῃσιν ἐπ' ὀφρύσι νεῦσε Κρονίων·}$$
$$\text{ἀμβρόσιαι δ' ἄρα χαῖται ἐπερρώσαντο ἄνακτος}$$
$$\text{κρατὸς ἀπ' ἀθανάτοιο· μέγαν δ' ἐλέλιξεν Ὄλυμπον.}^3$$

Dixit et avertens rosea cervice refulsit,
ambrosiaeque comae divinum vertice odorem

3 Ἦ καὶ...Ὄλυμπον Homer *Iliad* 1.528-30: "The son of Cronos spoke, and bowed his dark brow in assent, and the ambrosial locks waved from the king's immortal head; and he made great Olympus to quake"

spiravere; pedes vestis defluxit ad imos,
et vera incessu patuit dea. . . .[4]

Homer's persons are most of them godlike and terrible;
Vergil has scarce admitted any into his poem who are not
beautiful and has taken particular care to make his hero so.

. . . lumenque iuventae
purpureum et laetos oculis adflarat honores[5]

In a word, Homer fills his readers with sublime ideas and, I
believe, has raised the imagination of all the good poets that
have come after him. I shall only instance Horace, who
immediately takes fire at the first hint of any passage in the
Iliad or *Odyssey* and always rises above himself when he has
Homer in his view. Vergil has drawn together into his
Aeneid all the pleasing scenes that his subject is capable of
admitting and in his *Georgics* has given us a collection of the
most delightful landscapes that can be made out of fields
and woods, herds of cattle, and swarms of bees.

Ovid in his *Metamorphoses* has shown us how the imagination may be affected by what is strange. He describes a
miracle in every story and always gives us the sight of some
new creature at the end of it. His art consists chiefly in
well-timing his description before the first shape is quite
worn off and the new one perfectly finished, so that he
everywhere entertains us with something we never saw
before and shows monster after monster to the end of the
Metamorphoses.

If I were to name a poet that is a perfect master in all these
arts of working on the imagination, I think Milton may pass
for one. And if his *Paradise Lost* falls short of the *Aeneid* or
Iliad in this respect, it proceeds rather from the fault of the
language in which it is written than from any defect of
genius in the author. So divine a poem in English is like a
stately palace built of brick, where one may see architecture
in as great a perfection as in one of marble, though the

4 **Dixit . . . dea** Vergil *Aeneid* 1.402-5: "She spake, and as she
turned away, her roseate neck flashed bright. From her head her
ambrosial tresses breathed celestial fragrance; down to her feet fell
her raiment, and in her step she was revealed, a very goddess"
5 **lumenque . . . honores** Vergil *Aeneid* 1.590-1: ". . . with youth's
ruddy bloom, and on his eyes a joyous luster"

materials are of a coarser nature. But to consider it only as it regards our present subject, what can be conceived greater than the battle of angels, the majesty of Messiah, the stature and behavior of Satan and his peers? What more beautiful than Pandaemonium, Paradise, heaven, angels, Adam and Eve? What more strange than the creation of the world, the several metamorphoses of the fallen angels, and the surprising adventures that their leader meets with in his search after Paradise? No other subject could have furnished a poet with scenes so proper to strike the imagination, as no other poet could have painted those scenes in more strong and lively colors.

O

No. 418

[Pleasures of the imagination arising from the literary experience of terror and pity]

Monday, June 30, 1712

> . . . *ferat et rubus asper amomum.*—Verg.[1]

The pleasures of these secondary views of the imagination are of a wider and more universal nature than those it has when joined with sight; for not only what is great, strange, or beautiful, but anything that is disagreeable when looked upon pleases us in an apt description. Here, therefore, we must inquire after a new principle of pleasure, which is nothing else but the action of the mind which compares the ideas that arise from words with the ideas that arise from the objects themselves; and why this operation of the mind is attended with so much pleasure we have before considered. For this reason, therefore, the description of a dunghill is

1 ferat . . . amomum Vergil *Eclogues* 3.89: ". . . and the rough bramble bear spices"

pleasing to the imagination if the image be presented to our minds by suitable expressions, though perhaps this may be more properly called the pleasure of the understanding than of the fancy, because we are not so much delighted with the image that is contained in the description as with the aptness of the description to excite the image.

But if the description of what is little, common, or deformed be acceptable to the imagination, the description of what is great, surprising, or beautiful is much more so; because here we are not only delighted with comparing the representation with the original, but are highly pleased with the original itself. Most readers, I believe, are more charmed with Milton's description of Paradise than of hell; they are both, perhaps, equally perfect in their kind, but in the one the brimstone and sulphur are not so refreshing to the imagination as the beds of flowers and the wilderness of sweets in the other.

There is yet another circumstance which recommends a description more than all the rest, and that is if it represents to us such objects as are apt to raise a secret ferment in the mind of the reader and to work with violence upon his passions; for in this case we are at once warmed and enlightened, so that the pleasure becomes more universal and is several ways qualified to entertain us. Thus, as in painting, it is pleasant to look on the picture of any face where the resemblance is hit, but the pleasure increases if it be the picture of a face that is beautiful and is still greater if the beauty be softened with an air of melancholy or sorrow. The two leading passions that the more serious parts of poetry endeavor to stir up in us are terror and pity. And here, by the way, one would wonder how it comes to pass that such passions as are very unpleasant at all other times are very agreeable when excited by proper descriptions. It is not strange that we should take delight in such passages as are apt to produce hope, joy, admiration, love, or the like emotions in us, because they never rise in the mind without an inward pleasure that attends them. But how comes it to pass that we should take delight in being terrified or dejected by a description when we find so much uneasiness in the fear or grief that we receive from any other occasion?

If we consider, therefore, the nature of this pleasure, we shall find that it does not arise so properly from the description of what is terrible as from the reflection we make on ourselves at the time of reading it. When we look on such hideous objects, we are not a little pleased to think we are in no danger of them. We consider them at the same time as dreadful and harmless, so that the more frightful appearance they make, the greater is the pleasure we receive from the sense of our own safety. In short, we look upon the terrors of a description with the same curiosity and satisfaction that we survey a dead monster.

> . . . informe cadaver
> protrahitur. nequeunt expleri corda tuendo
> terribiles oculos, voltum villosaque saetis
> pectora semiferi atque exstinctos faucibus ignis.
> —Verg.[2]

It is for the same reason that we are delighted with the reflecting upon dangers that are past or in looking on a precipice at a distance which would fill us with a different kind of horror if we saw it hanging over our heads.

In the like manner, when we read of torments, wounds, deaths, and the like dismal accidents, our pleasure does not flow so properly from the grief that such melancholy descriptions give us as from the secret comparison which we make between ourselves and the person that suffers. Such representations teach us to set a just value upon our own condition and make us prize our good fortune which exempts us from the like calamities. This is, however, such a kind of pleasure as we are not capable of receiving when we see a person actually lying under the tortures that we meet with in a description, because in this case the object presses too close upon our senses and bears so hard upon us that it does not give us time or leisure to reflect on ourselves. Our thoughts are so intent upon the miseries of the sufferer that we cannot turn them upon our own happiness. Whereas, on the contrary, we consider the misfortunes we read in history

---

2 informe cadaver . . . ignis Vergil *Aeneid* 8.264-7: ". . . and the shapeless carcass is dragged forth. Men cannot sate their hearts with gazing on the terrible eyes, the face, and shaggy bristling chest of the brutish creature, and the quenched fires of his throat"

or poetry either as past or as fictitious, so that the reflection upon ourselves rises in us insensibly and overbears the sorrow we conceive for the sufferings of the afflicted.

But because the mind of man requires something more perfect in matter than what it finds there and can never meet with any sight in nature which sufficiently answers its highest ideas of pleasantness, or, in other words, because the imagination can fancy to itself things more great, strange, or beautiful than the eye ever saw and is still sensible of some defect in what it has seen, on this account it is the part of a poet to humor the imagination in its own notions by mending and perfecting nature where he describes a reality and by adding greater beauties than are put together in nature where he describes a fiction.

He is not obliged to attend her in the slow advances which she makes from one season to another or to observe her conduct in the successive production of plants and flowers. He may draw into his description all the beauties of the spring and autumn and make the whole year contribute something to render it the more agreeable. His rose trees, woodbines, and jessamines may flower together and his beds be covered at the same time with lilies, violets, and amaranths. His soil is not restrained to any particular set of plants, but is proper either for oaks or myrtles and adapts itself to the products of every climate. Oranges may grow wild in it, myrrh may be met with in every hedge, and if he thinks it proper to have a grove of spices, he can quickly command sun enough to raise it. If all this will not furnish out an agreeable scene, he can make several new species of flowers with richer scents and higher colors than any that grow in the gardens of nature. His consorts of birds may be as full and harmonious and his woods as thick and gloomy as he pleases. He is at no more expense in a long vista than a short one and can as easily throw his cascades from a precipice of half a mile high as from one of twenty yards. He has his choice of the winds and can turn the course of his rivers in all the variety of meanders that are most delightful to the reader's imagination. In a word, he has the modeling of nature in his own hands and may give her what charms he pleases, provided he does not reform her too much and run into absurdities by endeavoring to excel.

O

No. 419

[Pleasures of the imagination arising from "the fairy
way of writing"]

Tuesday, July 1, 1712

> *. . . mentis gratissimus error.*—Hor.[1]

There is a kind of writing wherein the poet quite loses sight
of nature and entertains his reader's imagination with the
characters and actions of such persons as have many of them
no existence but what he bestows on them. Such are fairies,
witches, magicians, demons, and departed spirits. This Mr.
Dryden calls "the fairy way of writing,"[2] which is, indeed,
more difficult than any other that depends on the poet's
fancy, because he has no pattern to follow in it and must
work altogether out of his own invention.

There is a very odd turn of thought required for this sort of
writing, and it is impossible for a poet to succeed in it who
has not a particular cast of fancy and an imagination naturally fruitful and superstitious. Besides this, he ought to be
very well versed in legends and fables, antiquated ro-
mances, and the traditions of nurses and old women, that he
may fall in with our natural prejudices and humor those
notions which we have imbibed in our infancy; for otherwise he will be apt to make his fairies talk like people of his
own species and not like other sets of beings who converse
with different objects and think in a different manner from
that of mankind:

1 **mentis . . . error** Horace *Epistles* 2.2.140: ". . . the dearest illu-
sion of my heart" 2 **Dryden calls "the fairy way of writing"**
Dedication of *King Arthur* (1691)

silvis deducti caveant me iudice Fauni,
ne velut innati triviis ac paene forenses
aut nimium teneris iuvenentur versibus . . .[3]

I do not say with Mr. Bayes[4] in *The Rehearsal* that spirits
must not be confined to speak sense, but it is certain their
sense ought to be a little discolored that it may may seem
particular and proper to the person and condition of the
speaker.

These descriptions raise a pleasing kind of horror in the
mind of the reader and amuse his imagination with the
strangeness and novelty of the persons who are represented
in them. They bring up into our memory the stories we have
heard in our childhood and favor those secret terrors and
apprehensions to which the mind of man is naturally subject. We are pleased with surveying the different habits and
behaviors of foreign countries; how much more must we be
delighted and surprised when we are led, as it were, into a
new creation and see the persons and manners of another
species? Men of cold fancies and philosophical dispositions
object to this kind of poetry that it has not probability
enough to affect the imagination. But to this it may be
answered that we are sure in general there are many intellectual beings in the world besides ourselves, and several
species of spirits that are subject to different laws and
economies from those of mankind. When we see, therefore,
any of these represented naturally, we cannot look upon the
representation as altogether impossible; nay, many are pre-
possessed with such false opinions as dispose them to believe these particular delusions. At least, we have all heard
so many pleasing relations in favor of them that we do not
care for seeing through the falsehood and willingly give
ourselves up to so agreeable an imposture.

The ancients have not much of this poetry among them,
for, indeed, almost the whole substance of it owes its

---

3 silvis deducti . . . versibus Horace *Ars Poetica* 244-6: "When the
Fauns are brought from the forest, they should, methinks, beware
of behaving as though born at the crossways and almost as dwelling
in the Forum, playing at times the young bloods with their maw-
kish verses . . ."   **4 Bayes** the dramatist burlesqued in the Duke of
Buckingham's *The Rehearsal* (1671)

original to the darkness and superstition of later ages when pious frauds were made use of to amuse mankind and frighten them into a sense of their duty. Our forefathers looked upon nature with more reverence and horror before the world was enlightened by learning and philosophy and loved to astonish themselves with the apprehensions of witchcraft, prodigies, charms, and enchantments. There was scarce a village in England that had not a ghost in it, the churchyards were all haunted, every large common had a circle of fairies belonging to it, and there was scarce a shepherd to be met with who had not seen a spirit.

Among all the poets of this kind our English are much the best by what I have yet seen, whether it be that we abound with more stories of this nature or that the genius of our country is fitter for this sort of poetry; for the English are naturally fanciful and very often disposed by that gloominess and melancholy of temper which is so frequent in our nation to many wild notions and visions to which others are not so liable.

Among the English, Shakespeare has incomparably excelled all others. That noble extravagance of fancy which he had in so great perfection thoroughly qualified him to touch this weak superstitious part of his reader's imagination and made him capable of succeeding where he had nothing to support him besides the strength of his own genius. There is something so wild and yet so solemn in the speeches of his ghosts, fairies, witches, and the like imaginary persons that we cannot forbear thinking them natural, though we have no rule by which to judge of them, and must confess if there are such beings in the world it looks highly probable they should talk and act as he has represented them.

There is another sort of imaginary beings that we sometimes meet with among the poets when the author represents any passion, appetite, virtue, or vice under a visible shape and makes it a person or an actor in his poem. Of this nature are the descriptions of Hunger and Envy in Ovid, of Fame in Vergil, and of Sin and Death in Milton. We find a whole creation of the like shadowy persons in Spenser, who had an admirable talent in representations of this kind. I have discoursed of these emblematical persons in former papers and shall therefore only mention them in this place. Thus we see how many ways poetry addresses itself to the imagination, as it has not only the whole circle of nature for its province but makes new worlds of its own, shows us persons that are not to be found in being, and represents even the faculties of the soul with her several virtues and vices in a sensible shape and character.

I shall in my two following papers consider in general how other kinds of writing are qualified to please the imagination, with which I intend to conclude this essay.

O

No. 420

[Pleasures of the imagination arising from scientific observation]

Wednesday, July 2, 1712

. . . *quocumque volent animum auditoris agunto.*—Hor.[1]

As the writers in poetry and fiction borrow their several materials from outward objects and join them together at their own pleasure, there are others who are obliged to follow nature more closely and to take entire scenes out of her. Such are historians, natural philosophers, travelers, geographers, and, in a word, all who describe visible objects of a real existence.

It is the most agreeable talent of an historian to be able to draw up his armies and fight his battles in proper expressions, to set before our eyes the divisions, cabals, and jealousies of great men, and to lead us step by step into the several actions and events of his history. We love to see the subject unfolding itself by just degrees and breaking upon

---

1 quocumque . . . agunto Horace *Ars Poetica* 100: "[Poems must] lead the hearer's soul where they will"

us insensibly, that so we may be kept in a pleasing suspense and have time given us to raise our expectations and to side with one of the parties concerned in the relation. I confess this shows more the art than the veracity of the historian, but I am only to speak of him as he is qualified to please the imagination. And in this respect Livy has, perhaps, excelled all who ever went before him or have written since his time. He describes everything in so lively a manner that his whole history is an admirable picture and touches on such proper circumstances in every story that his reader becomes a kind of spectator and feels in himself all the variety of passions which are correspondent to the several parts of the relation.

But among this set of writers there are none who more gratify and enlarge the imagination than the authors of the new philosophy, whether we consider their theories of the earth or heavens, the discoveries they have made by glasses, or any other of their contemplations on nature. We are not a little pleased to find every green leaf swarm with millions of animals that at their largest growth are not big enough to be visible. There is something very engaging to the fancy as well as to our reason in the treatises of metals, minerals, plants, and meteors. But when we survey the whole earth at once and the several planets that lie within its neighborhood, we are filled with a pleasing astonishment to see so many worlds hanging one above another and sliding round their axles in such an amazing pomp and solemnity. If after this we contemplate those wide fields of ether that reach in height as far as from Saturn to the fixed stars and run abroad almost to an infinitude, our imagination finds its capacity filled with so immense a prospect and puts itself upon the stretch to comprehend it. But if we yet rise higher and consider the fixed stars as so many vast oceans of flame that are each of them attended with a different set of planets and still discover new firmaments and new lights that are sunk farther in those unfathomable depths of ether so as not to be visible to the naked eye, we are lost in such a labyrinth of suns and worlds and confounded with the immensity and magnificence of nature.

Nothing is more pleasant to the fancy than to enlarge itself by degrees in its contemplation of the various proportions that its several objects bear to each other: when it compares the body of man to the bulk of the whole earth, the earth to the circle it describes round the sun, that circle to the sphere of the fixed stars, the sphere of the fixed stars to the circuit of the whole creation, the whole creation itself to the infinite space that is everywhere diffused about it; or when the imagination works downward and considers the bulk of a human body in respect of an animal a hundred times less than a mite, the particular limbs of such an animal, the different springs that actuate the limbs, the spirits that set these springs a-going, and the proportionable minuteness of these several parts before they have arrived at their full growth and perfection. But if, after all this, we take the least particle of these animal spirits and consider its capacity of being wrought into a world that shall contain within those narrow dimensions a heaven and earth, stars and planets, and every different species of living creatures in the same analogy and proportion they bear to each other in our own universe, such a speculation, by reason of its nicety, appears ridiculous to those who have not turned their thoughts that way, though at the same time it is founded on no less than the evidence of a demonstration. Nay, we might yet carry it farther and discover in the smallest particle of this little world a new inexhausted fund of matter capable of being spun out into another universe.

I have dwelt the longer on this subject because I think it may show us the proper limits as well as the defectiveness of our imagination, how it is confined to a very small quantity of space and immediately stopped in its operations when it endeavors to take in anything that is very great or very little. Let a man try to conceive the different bulk of an animal which is twenty from another which is a hundred times less than a mite, or to compare in his thoughts a length of a thousand diameters of the earth with that of a million, and he will quickly find that he has no different measures in his mind adjusted to such extraordinary degrees of grandeur or minuteness. The understanding, indeed, opens an infinite space on every side of us, but the imagination, after a few faint efforts, is immediately at a stand and finds herself swallowed up in the immensity of the void that surrounds it. Our reason can pursue a particle of matter through an infinite variety of divisions, but the fancy soon loses sight of it and feels in itself a kind of chasm that wants to be filled with matter of a more sensible bulk. We can neither widen nor contract the faculty to the dimensions of either extreme; the object is too big for our capacity when we would comprehend the circumference of a world and dwindles into nothing when we endeavor after the idea of an atom.

It is possible this defect of imagination may not be in the soul itself but as it acts in conjunction with the body. Perhaps there may not be room in the brain for such a variety of impressions, or the animal spirits may be incapable of figuring them in such a manner as is necessary to excite so very large or very minute ideas. However it be, we may well suppose that beings of a higher nature very much excel us in this respect, as it is probable the soul of man will be infinitely more perfect hereafter in this faculty as well as in all the rest—insomuch that, perhaps, the imagination will be able to keep pace with the understanding and to form in itself distinct ideas of all the different modes and quantities of space.

O

No. 421

[Pleasures of the imagination arising from rhetorical artifice]

Thursday, July 3, 1712

ignotis errare locis, ignota videre
flumina gaudebat, studio minuente laborem.—Ov.[1]

The pleasures of the imagination are not wholly confined to such particular authors as are conversant in material objects, but are often to be met with among the polite masters of morality, criticism, and other speculations abstracted

1   **ignotis . . . laborem**   Ovid *Metamorphoses* 4.294-5: ". . . delighting to wander in unknown lands and to see strange rivers, his eagerness making light of toil"

from matter, who, though they do not directly treat of the visible parts of nature, often draw from them their similitudes, metaphors, and allegories. By these allusions a truth in the understanding is as it were reflected by the imagination; we are able to see something like color and shape in a notion and to discover a scheme of thoughts traced out upon matter. And here the mind receives a great deal of satisfaction and has two of its faculties gratified at the same time while the fancy is busy in copying after the understanding and transcribing ideas out of the intellectual world into the material.

The great art of a writer shows itself in the choice of pleasing allusions, which are generally to be taken from the great or beautiful works of art or nature; for though whatever is new or uncommon is apt to delight the imagination, the chief design of an allusion being to illustrate and explain the passages of an author, it should always be borrowed from what is more known and common than the passages which are to be explained.

Allegories, when well chosen, are like so many tracks of light in a discourse that make everything about them clear and beautiful. A noble metaphor, when it is placed to an advantage, casts a kind of glory round it and darts a luster through a whole sentence. These different kinds of allusion are but so many different manners of similitude, and, that they may please the imagination, the likeness ought to be very exact or very agreeable, as we love to see a picture where the resemblance is just or the posture and air graceful. But we often find eminent writers very faulty in this respect; great scholars are apt to fetch their comparisons and allusions from the sciences in which they are most conversant, so that a man may see the compass of their learning in a treatise on the most indifferent subject. I have read a discourse upon love which none but a profound chemist could understand and have heard many a sermon that should only have been preached before a congregation of Cartesians.[2] On the contrary, your men of business usually have recourse to such instances as are too mean and familiar. They are for drawing the reader into a game of chess or tennis or for leading him from shop to shop in the cant of particular

2 **Cartesians** followers of the French philosopher René Descartes (1596-1650)

trades and employments. It is certain there may be found an
infinite variety of very agreeable allusions in both these
kinds, but for the generality the most entertaining ones lie
in the works of nature, which are obvious to all capacities
and more delightful than what is to be found in arts and
sciences.

It is this talent of affecting the imagination that gives an
embellishment to good sense and makes one man's compositions more agreeable than another's. It sets off all writings
in general, but is the very life and highest perfection of
poetry. Where it shines in an eminent degree, it has preserved several poems for many ages that have nothing else
to recommend them; and where all the other beauties are
present, the work appears dry and insipid if this single one
be wanting. It has something in it like creation: it bestows a
kind of existence and draws up to the reader's view several
objects which are not to be found in being; it makes additions to nature and gives a greater variety to God's works. In
a word, it is able to beautify and adorn the most illustrious
scenes in the universe or to fill the mind with more glorious
shows and apparitions than can be found in any part of it.

We have now discovered the several originals of those
pleasures that gratify the fancy, and here, perhaps, it would
not be very difficult to cast under their proper heads those
contrary objects that are apt to fill it with distaste and terror;
for the imagination is as liable to pain as pleasure. When the
brain is hurt by any accident or the mind disordered by
dreams or sickness, the fancy is overrun with wild dismal
ideas and terrified with a thousand hideous monsters of its
own framing.

> Eumenidum veluti demens videt agmina Pentheus,
> et solem geminum et duplices se ostendere Thebas,
> aut Agamemnonius scaenis agitatus Orestes
> armatam facibus matrem et serpentibus atris
> Cum fugit, ultricesque sedent in limine Dirae.—Ver.[3]

3 Eumenidum . . . Dirae Vergil *Aeneid* 4.469-73: "Even as raving
Pentheus sees the Furies' band, a double sun and twofold Thebes
rise to view; or as when Agamemnon's son, Orestes, driven over
the stage, flees from his mother, who is armed with brands and
black serpents, while at the doorway crouch the avenging Fiends"

There is not a sight in nature so mortifying as that of a distracted person when his imagination is troubled and his whole soul disordered and confused. Babylon in ruins is not so melancholy a spectacle. But to quit so disagreeable a subject, I shall only consider by way of conclusion what an infinite advantage this faculty gives an almighty being over the soul of man and how great a measure of happiness or misery we are capable of receiving from the imagination only.

We have already seen the influence that one man has over the fancy of another and with what ease he conveys into it a variety of imagery. How great a power, then, may we suppose lodged in him who knows all the ways of affecting the imagination, who can infuse what ideas he pleases and fill those ideas with terror and delight to what degree he thinks fit? He can excite images in the mind without the help of words and make scenes rise up before us and seem present to the eye without the assistance of bodies or exterior objects. He can transport the imagination with such beautiful and glorious visions as cannot possibly enter into our present conceptions or haunt it with such ghastly specters and apparitions as would make us hope for annihilation and think existence no better than a curse. In short, he can so exquisitely ravish or torture the soul through this single faculty as might suffice to make up the whole heaven or hell of any finite being.

This essay on the pleasures of the imagination having been published in separate papers, I shall conclude it with a table of the principal contents of each paper.

The Contents

Paper I

The perfection of our sight above our other senses. The pleasures of the imagination arise originally from sight. The pleasures of the imagination divided under two heads. The pleasures of the imagination in some respects equal to those of the understanding. The extent of the pleasures of the imagination. The advantages a man receives from a relish of these pleasures. In what respect they are preferable to those of the understanding.

Paper II

Three sources of all the pleasures of the imagination in our survey of outward objects. How what is great pleases the imagination. How what is new pleases the imagination. How what is beautiful in our own species pleases the imagination. How what is beautiful in general pleases the imagination. What other accidental causes may contribute to the heightening of these pleasures.

Paper III

Why the necessary cause of our being pleased with what is great, new, or beautiful unknown. Why the final cause more known and more useful. The final cause of our being pleased with what is great. The final cause of our being pleased with what is new. The final cause of our being pleased with what is beautiful in our own species. The final cause of our being pleased with what is beautiful in general.

Paper IV

The works of nature more pleasant to the imagination than those of art. The works of nature still more pleasant the more they resemble those of art. The works of art more pleasant the more they resemble those of nature. Our English plantations and gardens considered in the foregoing light.

Paper V

Of architecture as it affects the imagination. Greatness in architecture relates either to the bulk or to the manner. Greatness of bulk in the ancient Oriental buildings. The ancient accounts of these buildings confirmed: (1) from the advantages for raising such works in the first ages of the world and in the Eastern climates; (2) from several of them which are still extant. Instances how greatness of manner affects the imagination. A French author's observation on this subject. Why concave and convex figures give a greatness of manner to works of architecture. Everything that pleases the imagination in architecture is either great, beautiful, or new.

Paper VI

The secondary pleasures of the imagination. The several sources of these pleasures (statuary, painting, description, and music) compared together. The final cause of our receiving pleasure from these several sources. Of descriptions in particular. The power of words over the imagination. Why one reader more pleased with descriptions than another.

Paper VII

How a whole set of ideas hang together, etc. A natural cause assigned for it. How to perfect the imagination of a writer. Who among the ancient poets had this faculty in its greatest perfection. Homer excelled in imagining what is great, Vergil in imagining what is beautiful, Ovid in imagining what is new. Our own countryman Milton very perfect in all three respects.

Paper VIII

Why anything that is unpleasant to behold pleases the imagination when well described. Why the imagination receives a more exquisite pleasure from the description of what is great, new, or beautiful. This pleasure still heightened if what is described raises passion in the mind. Disagreeable passions pleasing when raised by apt descriptions. Why terror and grief are pleasing to the mind when excited by descriptions. A particular advantage the writers in poetry and fiction have to please the imagination. What liberties are allowed them.

Paper IX

Of that kind of poetry which Mr. Dryden calls "the fairy way of writing." How a poet should be qualified for it. The pleasures of the imagination that arise from it. In this respect, why the moderns excel the ancients. Why the English excel the moderns. Who the best among the English. Of emblematical persons.

Paper X

What authors please the imagination who have nothing to do with fiction. How history pleases the imagination.

How the authors of the new philosophy please the imagination. The bounds and defects of the imagination. Whether these defects are essential to the imagination.

Paper XI

How those please the imagination who treat of subjects abstracted from matter by allusions taken from it. What allusions most pleasing to the imagination. Great writers how faulty in this respect. Of the art of imagining in general. The imagination capable of pain as well as pleasure. In what degree the imagination is capable either of pain or pleasure.

O

DRAMATIC REFORM

No. 446

[Licentiousness in the drama and the need for supervision of the theaters]

Friday, August 1, 1712

quid deceat, quid non, quo virtus, quo ferat error.—Hor.[1]

Since two or three writers of comedy who are now living have taken their farewell of the stage, those who succeed them, finding themselves incapable of rising up to their wit, humor, and good sense, have only imitated them in some of those loose unguarded strokes in which they complied with the corrupt taste of the more vicious part of their audience. When persons of a low genius attempt this kind of writing, they know no difference between being merry and being lewd. It is with an eye to some of these degenerate compositions that I have written the following discourse.

Were our English stage but half so virtuous as that of the Greeks or Romans, we should quickly see the influence of it in the behavior of all the politer part of mankind. It would not be fashionable to ridicule religion or its professors, the man of pleasure would not be the complete gentleman,

---

1 quid deceat . . . error Horace *Ars Poetica* 308: "What befits him and what not; whither the right course leads and whither the wrong"

vanity would be out of countenance, and every quality which is ornamental to human nature would meet with that esteem which is due to it.

If the English stage were under the same regulations the Athenian was formerly, it would have the same effect that had in recommending the religion, the government, and public worship of its country. Were our plays subject to proper inspections and limitations, we might not only pass away several of our vacant hours in the highest entertainments, but should always rise from them wiser and better than we sat down to them.

It is one of the most unaccountable things in our age that the lewdness of our theater should be so much complained of, so well exposed, and so little redressed. It is to be hoped that sometime or other we may be at leisure to restrain the licentiousness of the theater and make it contribute its assistance to the advancement of morality and to the reformation of the age. As matters stand at present, multitudes are shut out from this noble diversion by reason of those abuses and corruptions that accompany it. A father is often afraid that his daughter should be ruined by those entertainments which were invented for the accomplishment and refining of human nature. The Athenian and Roman plays were written with such a regard to morality that Socrates used to frequent the one and Cicero the other.

It happened once indeed that Cato[2] dropped into the Roman theater when the Floralia[3] were to be represented, and as in that performance, which was a kind of religious ceremony, there were several indecent parts to be acted, the people refused to see them whilst Cato was present. Martial[4] on this hint made the following epigram, which we must suppose was applied to some grave friend of his that had been accidentally present at some such entertainment.

> Nosses iocosae dulce cum sacrum Florae
> festosque lusus et licentiam volgi,
> cur in theatrum, Cato severe, venisti?
> an ideo tantum veneras, ut exires?

2 **Cato** Marcus Porcinus Cato, the Elder (234-149 B.C.), famous for the reformation of moral standards   3 **Floralia** festival in honor of Flora during which mimes were performed   4 **Martial** *Epigrams* 1. *Praefatio (ex.)*

> Why dost thou come, great censor of thy age,
> To see the loose diversions of the stage?
> With awful countenance and brow severe,
> What in the name of goodness dost thou here?
> See the mixed crowd! How giddy, lewd, and vain!
> Didst thou come in but to go out again?

An accident of this nature might happen once in an age among the Greeks or Romans, but they were too wise and good to let the constant nightly entertainment be of such a nature that people of the most sense and virtue could not be at it. Whatever vices are represented upon the stage, they ought to be so marked and branded by the poet as not to appear either laudable or amiable in the person who is tainted with them. But if we look into the English comedies above mentioned, we would think they were formed upon a quite contrary maxim and that this rule, though it held good upon the heathen stage, was not to be regarded in Christian theaters. There is another rule likewise which was observed by authors of antiquity and which these modern geniuses have no regard to, and that was never to choose an improper subject for ridicule. Now a subject is improper for ridicule if it is apt to stir up horror and commiseration rather than laughter. For this reason we do not find any comedy in so polite an author as Terence[5] raised upon the violations of the marriage bed. The falsehood of the wife or husband has given occasion to noble tragedies, but a Scipio[6] or Laelius[7] would have looked upon incest or murder to have been as proper subjects for comedy. On the contrary, cuckoldom is the basis of most of our modern plays. If an alderman appears upon the stage, you may be sure it is in order to be cuckolded. A husband that is a little grave or elderly generally meets with the same fate. Knights and baronets, country squires, and justices of the quorum[8] come up to town for

---

5 **Terence** Publius Terentius Afer (190?-159 B.C.)   6 **Scipio** Publius Cornelius Scipio, known as Scipio Africanus Minor (ca. 185-129 B.C.)   7 **Laelius** Gaius Laelius Sapiens (b. ca. 186 B.C.), friend of Scipio   8 **justices of the quorum** certain justices of the peace whose presence was necessary to constitute a bench (*OED*)

no other purpose. I have seen poor Dogget[9] cuckolded in all these capacities. In short, our English writers are as frequently severe upon this innocent, unhappy creature, commonly known by the name of a cuckold, as the ancient comic writers were upon an eating parasite or a vainglorious soldier.

At the same time the poet so contrives his matters that the two criminals are the favorites of the audience. We sit still and wish well to them through the whole play, are pleased when they meet with proper opportunities, and are out of humor when they are disappointed. The truth of it is, the accomplished gentleman upon the English stage is the person that is familiar with other men's wives and indifferent to his own, as the fine woman is generally a composition of sprightliness and falsehood. I do not know whether it proceeds from barrenness of invention, depravation of manners, or ignorance of mankind, but I have often wondered that our ordinary poets cannot frame to themselves the idea of a fine man that is not a whoremaster or a fine woman that is not a jilt.

I have sometimes thought of compiling a system of ethics out of the writings of these corrupt poets under the title of *Stage Morality*. But I have been diverted from this thought by a project which has been executed by an ingenious gentleman of my acquaintance. He has composed, it seems, the history of a young fellow who has taken all his notions of the world from the stage and who has directed himself in every circumstance of his life and conversation by the maxims and examples of the fine gentleman in English comedies. If I can prevail upon him to give me a copy of this new-fashioned novel, I will bestow on it a place in my works and question not but it may have as good an effect upon the drama as *Don Quixote* had upon romance.

C

9 **Dogget** Thomas Dogget (ca. 1670-1721), English comic actor

Bibliography

EDITIONS

Tickell, Thomas, ed., *The Works of the Right Honourable Joseph Addison, Esq.*, 4 vols. (London, 1721).

Aitken, George A., ed., *The Spectator*, 8 vols. (London, 1898).

Smith, G. Gregory, ed., *The Spectator*, 4 vols. (Everyman's Library, New York, 1945).

Bond, Donald F., ed., *The Spectator*, 5 vols. (Oxford, 1965).

BIOGRAPHIES

Tickell, Thomas, Biographical preface in *The Works of Addison*, Vol. I (London, 1721).

Johnson, Samuel, *Lives of the English Poets: Addison*, ed. G. Birkbeck Hill, Vol. II (Oxford, 1905).

Smithers, Peter, *The Life of Joseph Addison*, 2d ed. (Oxford, 1968).

CRITICAL STUDIES

Abrams, M. H., *The Mirror and the Lamp: Romantic Theory and the Critical Tradition* (New York, 1953).

Atkins, J. W. H., *English Literary Criticism: Seventeenth and Eighteenth Centuries* (London, 1951).

Bate, Walter Jackson, *From Classic to Romantic: Premises of*

Taste in Eighteenth-Century England (Cambridge, Mass., 1946).

Bloom, Edward A., and Lillian D., *Joseph Addison's Sociable Animal* (Providence, 1971).

Chapin, Chester F., *Personification in Eighteenth-Century Poetry* (New York, 1955).

Elioseff, Lee Andrew, *The Cultural Milieu of Addison's Literary Criticism* (Austin, 1963).

Friedman, Albert B., "Addison's Ballad Papers and the Reaction to Metaphysical Wit," *Comparative Literature*, XII (1960), 1-13.

Friedman, Albert B., *The Ballad Revival: Studies in the Influence of Popular on Sophisticated Poetry* (Chicago, 1961).

Fussell, Paul, *The Rhetorical World of Augustan Humanism* (Oxford, 1965).

Gray, Charles Harold, *Theatrical Criticism in London to 1795* (New York, 1931).

Havens, Raymond Dexter, *The Influence of Milton on English Poetry* (Cambridge, Mass., 1922).

Hooker, Edward Niles, ed., *The Critical Works of John Dennis*, 2 vols. (Baltimore, 1939, 1943); includes extensive editorial commentary.

Hooker, Edward Niles, "Pope on Wit: The *Essay on Criticism*," *The Seventeenth Century: Studies in the History of English Thought and Literature from Bacon to Pope*, by Richard Foster Jones and others (Stanford, 1951), pp. 225-46.

Kaufman, Paul, "Heralds of Original Genius," *Essays in Memory of Barrett Wendell* (Cambridge, Mass., 1926), pp. 191-217.

Kliger, Samuel, *The Goths in England* (Cambridge, Mass., 1952).

Lewis, C. S., "Addison," in *Essays on the Eighteenth Century Presented to David Nichol Smith in Honour of His Seventieth Birthday* (Oxford, 1945), pp. 1-14.

Longueil, Alfred E., "The Word 'Gothic' in Eighteenth-Century Criticism," *Modern Language Notes*, XXXVIII (1923), 453-60.

Lovejoy, Arthur O., *Essays in the History of Ideas* (Baltimore, 1948).

MacLean, Kenneth, *John Locke and English Literature of the Eighteenth Century* (New Haven, 1936).

Monk, Samuel H., *The Sublime: A Study of Critical Theories in Eighteenth-Century England* (New York, 1935).

Nicolson, Marjorie Hope, *Mountain Gloom and Mountain Glory: The Development of the Aesthetics of the Infinite* (Ithaca, 1959).

Rothstein, Eric, *Restoration Tragedy: Form and the Process of Change* (Madison, 1967).

Stewart, Keith, "The Ballad and the *Genres*," *ELH: A Journal of English Literary History*, XXIV (1957), 120-37.

Thorpe, Clarence DeWitt, "Addison's Contribution to Criticism," *The Seventeenth Century: Studies in the History of English Thought and Literature from Bacon to Pope*, by Richard Foster Jones and others (Stanford, 1951), pp. 316-29.

Thorpe, James E., Introduction, *Milton Criticism: Selections from Four Centuries* (London, 1956).

Tuveson, Ernest Lee, *The Imagination as a Means of Grace* (Berkeley and Los Angeles, 1960).

Tyre, Richard H., "Versions of Poetic Justice in the Early Eighteenth Century," *Studies in Philology*, LIV (1957), 29-44.

Wellek, René, *The Rise of English Literary History* (Chapel Hill, 1941).

Wimsatt, William Kurtz, Jr., Introduction, *Parodies of Ballad Criticism (1711-1787)*, Augustan Reprint Society, No. 63, 1957.

Wimsatt, William Kurtz, Jr., and Cleanth Brooks, *Literary Criticism: A Short History* (New York, 1957).

Woolf, Virginia, "Addison," *The Common Reader* (London, 1925), pp. 132-45.